SpringerBriefs in Computer Science

Bahadir Karasulu · Serdar Korukoglu

Performance Evaluation Software

Moving Object Detection and Tracking in Videos

 Springer

Bahadir Karasulu
Department of Computer Engineering
Canakkale Onsekiz Mart University
Canakkale
Turkey

Serdar Korukoglu
Department of Computer Engineering
Ege University
Bornova, Izmir
Turkey

ISSN 2191-5768   ISSN 2191-5776 (electronic)
ISBN 978-1-4614-6533-1   ISBN 978-1-4614-6534-8   (eBook)
DOI 10.1007/978-1-4614-6534-8
Springer New York Heidelberg Dordrecht London

Library of Congress Control Number: 2013934014

Printed on acid-free paper

Springer is part of Springer Science+Business Media (www.springer.com)

Dedicated to Karasulu and Korukoglu families...

Dedicated to Karasulu and Korukoglu families...

Preface

Moving object detection and/or tracking (D&T) is a wide-scope research domain in the computer vision area. This book introduces a software approach for the real-time evaluation and performance comparison of the methods specialized for moving object D&T in video processing. Digital video content analysis is an important item for multimedia content-based indexing (MCBI), content-based video retrieval (CBVR), and visual surveillance systems. There are some frequently used generic algorithms for video object D&T in the literature, such as Background Subtraction (BS), Continuously Adaptive Mean-shift (CMS), Optical Flow (OF), etc. An important problem for performance evaluation is the absence of any stable and flexible software for comparison of different algorithms.

In this frame, we have designed and implemented the software for the performance comparison and evaluation of well-known video object D&T algorithms at the same platform. This software is able to compare them with the same metrics in real-time and at the same platform, and works as an automatic and/or semi-automatic test environment in real-time, which uses the image and video processing essentials, e.g., morphological operations and filters, and ground-truth (GT) XML data files, charting/plotting capabilities, etc. Along with the comprehensive literature survey of the above-mentioned video object D&T algorithms, this book also covers the technical details of our performance benchmark software as well as a case study on people D&T for the functionality of the software.

This book is organized into six chapters. Chapter 1 introduces our study and its main contribution to the literature. Chapter 2 reviews the commonly implemented object D&T algorithms (i.e., methods) and their applications in the literature. Chapter 3 represents the details of our software approach to performance evaluation of moving object D&T, and architecture overview for our software. Chapter 4 provides detailed information about performance evaluation and metrics used in the proposed software approach. Chapter 5 declares the details of video datasets used in our study and the experimental results. Furthermore, Chap. 5 shows the analysis of quantitative performance results both using statistical and algorithmic analysis. The final chapter of the book provides the conclusions.

Serdar Korukoglu is a full-time professor of Computer Engineering Department at Ege University, Izmir, Turkey. He received his B.S. degree in Industrial Engineering, M.Sc. in Applied Statistics, and Ph.D. in Computer Engineering from

Ege University, Izmir, Turkey. He was a visiting research fellow in 1985 in Reading University of England.

Bahadir Karasulu is a full-time assistant professor of the Computer Engineering Department at Canakkale Onsekiz Mart University, Canakkale, Turkey. In 2003, he graduated from the Science and Arts Faculty—Physics Department at Kocaeli University, Kocaeli, Turkey. Afterwards, in 2006, he completed an M.Sc. thesis study titled 'Application of Parallel Computing Technique to Monte Carlo Simulation' in the Computer Engineering Department of Maltepe University, Istanbul, Turkey. In 2010, he obtained his Ph.D. degree in Computer Engineering Department of Ege University, Izmir, Turkey. His Ph.D. thesis study is titled 'A Simulated Annealing based Performance Optimization Approach for Moving Object Detection and Tracking in Videos'. His research interests include artificial intelligence, computer vision, pattern recognition, as well as distributed and parallel computing, simulation, and optimization.

Much of the essential material in this book is based on the Ph.D. dissertation of Bahadir Karasulu and a subsequent journal article, which is published in the journal of Multimedia Tools and Applications, i.e., a comprehensive international journal of Springer Science+Business Media LLC (DOI: 10.1007/s11042-010-0591-2).

Canakkale, Turkey, September 2012   Bahadir Karasulu
Izmir, Turkey   Serdar Korukoglu

Acknowledgments

The authors would like to thank their families for encouraging them during the writing of this book. In addition, Bahadir Karasulu is especially grateful to Bora Karasulu for his valuable comments on this book. The authors are also grateful for the assistance provided by Courtney Clark and the publication team at SpringerBriefs.

Acknowledgments

Contents

Acronyms

ABP	Area-based precision
ABR	Area-based recall
Adj. MS	Adjusted mean square
Adj. SS	Adjusted sum of squares
AF	Average fragmentation
ARDA	Advanced Research and Development Activity
ATA	Average tracking accuracy
ATE	Automatic test environment
ATP	Area-thresholded precision
ATR	Area-thresholded recall
BF	Bilateral filtering
BS	Background Subtraction
CAMSGPF	CAMShift guided particle filter
CAMShift	Continuously Adaptive Mean-shift
CAVIAR	Context Aware Vision using Image-based Active Recognition
CBVR	Content-based video retrieval
CCA	Connected component analysis
CMS	Continuously Adaptive Mean-shift
CPD	Color probability distribution
CSM	Contour saliency map
CT	Computed Tomography
CVML	Computer Vision Markup Language
DF	Degrees of freedom
D&T	Detection and tracking
DTO	Detected object
FA	False alarm
FAR	False alarm rate
FN	False negative
FP	False positive
GM	Gaussian mixture
GT	Ground-truth
GTO	Ground-truth object
GUI	Graphical user interface

HS	Horn-Schunck
HSI	Hue-Saturation-Intensity
HSV	Hue-Saturation-Value
INRIA	Institut National de Recherche en Informatique et en Automatique
KLT	Kanade–Lucas–Tomasi
LK	Lucas–Kanade
LoG	Laplacian of Gaussian
MCBI	Multimedia content-based indexing
MD	Missed detect
MERL-PEP	Mitsubishi Electric Research Laboratories Performance Evaluation Platform
MLP	Multilayer perceptron
MoG	Mixture of Gaussian
MS	Mean-shift
MSE	Mean square error
MSEPF	Mean-shift embedded particle filter
MSF	Mean-shift filtering
OBM	Orientation-based measure
OCA	Object count accuracy
OCBF2	Object count-based F2 measure
ODViS	Open Development for Video Surveillance
OF	Optical flow
OpenCV	Open source Computer Vision library
PA	Positional accuracy
PBF1	Pixel-based F1 measure
PBM	Position-based measure
PBP	Pixel-based precision
PBR	Pixel-based recall
PDF	Probability density function
PETS	Performance Evaluation of Tracking and Surveillance
PF	Particle filter
RAA	Running average alpha
RADC	Running average difference computation
RBF	Radial basis function
RGB	Red-Green-Blue
ROC	Receiver operating characteristic
ROI	Region of interest
SATE	Semi-automatic test environment
SBM	Size-based measure
SFDA	Sequence frame detection accuracy
STDA	Sequence tracking detection accuracy
TDA	Tracking detection accuracy
TDR	Tracker detection rate
TempF3	Temporal F3 measure
TP	True positive

TPR	True positive rate
TSL	Tint–Saturation–Luminance
UML	Unified Modeling Language
VACE	Video Analysis and Content Extraction
ViCamPEv	Video & Camera Performance Evaluation tool
VIPeR	Viewpoint Invariant Pedestrian Recognition
XML	eXtensible Markup Language

Chapter 1
Introduction

Abstract This chapter comprises three sections. The first section represents the scope of this book. The second section introduces the related works on the issue of moving object detection and tracking (D&T) in videos. Also, the main objective for moving object D&T and main scenarios for visual surveillance applications is given in this chapter. The moving object D&T methods in video processing are categorized in some ways where their respective aspects are taken as the basis of the D&T process. In the second section, the basis of performance and evaluation of moving object D&T process is declared, such as with-ground-truth and without-ground-truth evaluation. In addition, commonly used video datasets, their tools, and some systems for object D&T are briefly introduced. This chapter ends with a third section focused on the main contribution of the study given in this book.

Keywords Object detection · Object tracking · Video dataset

1.1 Scope

In current visual surveillance systems, the necessity of moving object detection and tracking (D&T) methods become more and more an essential aspect, as upcoming new technologies need to be integrated on demand and on-the-fly into visual surveillance systems. In computer science, video processing is an important research area. In common multimedia systems, 2D videos are used in object segmentation and D&T processes, which are forming the basis for information retrieval, content-based indexing, people tracking, visual surveillance systems (e.g., distributed cross-camera systems), 3DTV applications, and traffic monitoring [1–3], also, they can be captured from either a stationary camera or moving camera [4]. Moving object detection from video is the essential step for more complex processes, such as video object tracking and video retrieval. In this frame, video object tracking can be defined as the process of segmenting the object(s) of interest from a given video scene. The main objective of moving object D&T is to locate foreground object(s); these objects can also be tracked, which are used for further analysis of the video context. The main challenge that lies in the moving object D&T is information loss [5], which is caused by complex background clusters, different illumination changes, shadows, occlusion, time-varied background, etc. In order to extract useful and meaningful context information, the object D&T process should keep track of the object's motion (i.e., trajectory), orientation, and moving speed.

This book is organized as follows. Chapter 2 describes the most commonly implemented object D&T algorithms (i.e., methods) and their applications. Chapter 3 shows the details of our software approach to performance evaluation of moving object D&T, and architecture overview for our ViCamPEv (abbreviation for Video & Camera Performance Evaluation tool) software. This software is able to compare the object D&T methods with the same metrics in real-time and at the same platform, and works as an automatic and/or semi-automatic test environment in real-time, which uses image and video processing essentials, e.g., morphological operations and filters, and ground-truth (GT) XML data files, charting/plotting capabilities, etc. Chapter 4 provides detailed information about performance evaluation and metrics used in the proposed approach. Chapter 5 declares the details of dataset used in our study and the experimental results. In addition, Chap. 5 represents the analysis of quantitative performance results using both statistical and algorithmic analysis. Chapter 6 concludes the book.

1.2 Related Work

In the last decades, many methods have been developed and reported for object D&T from video. According to Liu et al. [4], these methods can be categorized into three approaches; contour-based [6–8], orientation-based [9, 10], and distribution-based [11–16]. In the study by Karasulu and Korukoglu [17], several methods for object D&T were also implemented at the same platform. In addition, Huang et al. [18] categorized the object D&T approaches, such as feature-based [19–22], inter-frame difference-based [12, 23, 24], and template-based detection [25, 26].

For visual surveillance applications, there are two main situations, namely indoor and outdoor scenarios. According to Lei and Xu [27], in indoor scenarios, the monitoring space is normally constrained, and the camera-object distance is relatively small. This situation results in relatively large-sized objects with clearer appearance. Therefore, an appearance model can be used to address effectively dynamic and stationary occlusions and to enable consistent labeling of objects [28]. In outdoor scenarios, it often operates in unconstrained and complex environments, namely shape and size of objects are different from each other, and these subjects vary in the field of view of the camera. The weather conditions are changeable with the time of day, or motion characteristics of given objects may exhibit sudden changes. Moving objects may disappear and reappear in a given scene [27].

For computer vision problems, object D&T algorithms usually fail while dealing with the above-mentioned complex scenarios. These scenarios are given in the literature such as occlusions in crowded pedestrian scenes, on the sports field, shopping center, or parking lots, etc. However, object recognition algorithms rarely give good accuracy results on well-predefined (i.e., annotated) datasets [17, 29]. In order to make accurate performance measurements and evaluation, researchers need to use suitable datasets. The context of these datasets (i.e., object's property) is manually predefined (i.e., pre-annotated) by an expert human. Furthermore, ground-truth (GT) data of the datasets must be the optimal output for exactly what the algorithm is expected to generate [17, 30, 31]. The GT is treated as a reference (i.e., golden standard) for evaluation of performance of given D&T methods. There is a variety of methods dedicated to generic object D&T in video processing like Background Subtraction (BS) [23, 32, 33], Mean-shift (MS) and/or Continuously Adaptive Mean-shift (CMS) [34–36], Optical Flow (OF) [37, 38], etc.

According to Huang et al. [18], the basic inter-frame difference-based detection is BS method, which is used in object trackers. In some studies [12, 23, 24], the values taken by individual pixels over time are statistically modeled. According to these studies, the object detection is performed by finding those pixels with values that deviate from given statistical model for the background in given scene. The OF is an orientation-based approach, which can accurately detect the motion direction, but is sensitive to illumination changes. Also, there are many feature-based approaches, which are based on finding corresponding features in successive frames. These features are generally corners, colors, and contours.

These methods and their modifications are used for D&T process of people, text, face, and/or vehicle. According to Kasturi et al. [39], in video processing, some empirical evaluation of generic object D&T algorithm(s) present an overabundance of metrics specialized to measure different aspects of performance [17]. These metrics are useful for error analysis. However, they do not provide an effective measure for object D&T performance [17, 40]. In this frame, the comparison of any two systems or algorithms is a more challenging issue. For overcoming this problem, researchers need to use a software tool and with its help test the efficiency, robustness, and accuracy of an object D&T algorithm. In addition, similar specific frameworks and platforms exist in the literature [17, 39, 41, 42].

Furthermore, previous studies are pretty much focused on the issue of moving object D&T in videos. The issue of evaluating the total performance of video surveillance systems is becoming important. In some studies, this issue was reviewed [17, 43–45]. Performance evaluation is a robustness and goodness test for object D&T algorithms of methods. Some commonly implemented methods and their algorithms for performance evaluation and appropriate ways for performance measurement of moving object D&T are reviewed in this book. In addition, the performance evaluation can be divided into two major types: with-ground-truth or without-ground-truth evaluation. In our study, we are interested in with-ground-truth evaluation. In with-ground-truth evaluation, object D&T conventional metrics can be divided into two groups: Frame-based and Object-based D&T metrics [17, 45].

For testing of an algorithm of object D&T methods, a standard format (mostly in eXtensible Markup Language, XML) of GT data for videos is usually needed. The D&T results of some performance evaluation systems were published in their websites and in related papers. In this way, researchers achieve a comparison for some equivalent and different systems or methods by these results [17]. Commonly used GT generation (i.e., annotation) tools for Context Aware Vision using Image-based Active Recognition (CAVIAR) [17, 46], Viewpoint Invariant Pedestrian Recognition (VIPeR) [17, 47], Open Development for Video Surveillance (ODViS) [17, 48], and others are available in the literature. Some of these tools have their own video datasets as well. Indoor and/or city center surveillance and retail applications (e.g., people tracking) are addressed in CAVIAR project, which uses an annotation tool based on the AviTrack [17, 49] project. The GT XML files are used in CAVIAR, which are based on Computer Vision Markup Language (CVML) [17, 50]. Baumann et al. [17, 43] talked about several video performance evaluation projects [17, 51, 52].

There are huge frameworks on performance evaluation issue of video surveillance systems, such as Performance Evaluation of Tracking and Surveillance (PETS) [17, 53] and Video Analysis and Content Extraction (VACE) [17, 54]. The VACE program is supported by Advanced Research and Development Activity (ARDA). VACE has some frame-based and object-based D&T metrics for performance evaluation. In the literature, there are some other software and environments for object detection, tracking, and/or testing. However, their main problem is absence of software stability and flexibility for comparison of different methods by using the same metrics at the same platform in real-time. This kind of software is generally made for XML GT file using and loading processes, which are seamlessly from end-user. At the end of these processes, the end-user sees only the performance results [17].

Mitsubishi Electric Research Laboratories Performance Evaluation Platform for Object Tracking Methods (MERL-PEP) is a good example for complete performance evaluation platform for object D&T methods [17, 41]. They have declared the goal of the project in their website. The goal is to develop a complete performance evaluation platform for object D&T systems. The CellTrack is another good example of object D&T software tool, but it is a specific-area (i.e., bioinformatics) tool. In addition, it does not evaluate the performance of object D&T. According to Sacan et al. [17, 42], CellTrack is a cross-platform, self-contained, and extensible software package for motility analysis and cell tracking (i.e., biological process). Sacan et al. [42] have implemented a novel edge-based method for sensitive tracking of the cell boundaries, and constructed an ensemble of methods.

Huang et al. [18] proposed a real-time object D&T system for outdoor night visual surveillance. The algorithm of their system's basis is based on contrast analysis. In the first stage, the contrast in local change over time is used to detect potential moving objects. Then motion prediction and spatial nearest neighbor data association are used to suppress false alarms (FA). The experimental results on real scenes show that their algorithm is effective for nighttime object D&T process.

1.3 Main Contribution

In this study, we proposed a performance analysis and object D&T software [17]. It is developed for performance evaluation of most frequently used D&T algorithms in video processing. In this study, our contribution is to develop a software for performance evaluation. This is different from non-real-time similar works, as it compares performance measurements for moving object D&T in videos amongst different algorithms in real-time. In this frame, an important problem is the absence of stable and flexible software for comparison of different algorithms (or methods).

In this book, we declare our object D&T performance evaluation software details and its usefulness in the performance evaluation research area. Furthermore, a case study on people D&T is presented for showing the functionality of the software. This software is able to compare video object D&T methods using the same metrics in real-time and at the same platform. From the point of view of problem solution, our software provides general purpose image processing, morphological operations and some filters, object D&T, and performance evaluation in real-time at the same platform [17]. In addition, a comprehensive literature survey of the related methods of video object D&T is covered in this book.

Chapter 2
Moving Object Detection and Tracking in Videos

Abstract This chapter provides four sections. The first section introduces the moving object D&T infrastructure and basis of some methods for object detection and tracking (D&T) in videos. In object D&T applications, there is manual or automatic D&T process. Also, the image features, such as color, shape, texture, contours, and motion can be used to track the moving object(s) in videos. The detailed information for moving object detection and well-known trackers are presented in this section as well. In second section, the background subtraction (BS) method and its applications are given in details. The third section declares the details for Mean-shift (MS), Mean-shift filtering (MSF), and continuously adaptive Mean-shift (CMS or CAMShift) methods and their applications. In fourth section, the details for the optical flow (OF), the corner detection through feature points, and OF-based trackers are given in details.

Keywords Background subtraction · Mean-shift · CAMShift · Mean-shift filtering · Optical flow

2.1 Introduction

In video processing, a video can be represented with some hierarchical structure units, such as scene, shot and frame. Also, video frame is the lowest level in the hierarchical structure. The content-based video browsing and retrieval, video-content analysis use these structure units. In video retrieval, generally, video applications must first partition a given video sequence into video shots. A video shot is defined as an image or video frame sequence that presents continuous action. The frames in a video shot are captured from a single operation of one camera. The complete video sequence is generally formed by joining two or more video shots [55, 56].

According to Koprinska and Carrato [56], there are two basic types of video shot transitions, namely abrupt and gradual. Abrupt transitions (i.e., cuts) are sim-

B. Karasulu and S. Korukoglu, *Performance Evaluation Software*, SpringerBriefs
in Computer Science, DOI: 10.1007/978-1-4614-6534-8_2, © The Author(s) 2013

plest form, which occur in a single frame when stopping and restarting the camera. Although many kinds of cinematic effects could be applied to artificially combine two or more video shots. Therefore, the fades and dissolves are most often used to create gradual transitions. A slow decrease in brightness resulting in a black frame is a fade-out. In addition, a fade-in is a gradual increase in intensity starting from a black image. However, dissolves show one image superimposed on the other as the frames of the first video shot get dimmer and those of the second one get brighter [56].

In Camara-Chavez et al. study [55], they expressed that video shots can be effectively considered as the smallest indexing unit where no change in the scene content can be perceived. In addition, the higher level concepts are often constructed by combining and analyzing the inter- and intra-shot relationships. For a video or multimedia indexing, or editing application, each video shot can be generally represented by key frames and indexed according to the spatial and temporal features [55, 57]. In the literature, several content-based retrieval systems for organizing and managing video databases have been already proposed [56]. In Fig. 2.1, a schematic for content-based retrieval of video databases is shown. In this schematic, one can see that video shots cover key frames, and above mentioned temporal and spatial features are extracted from these video shots as well. In addition, the end-users may interact with such a retrieval system and those interactions lead to the indexing and annotation processes via browse, search, edit, or analyze operations.

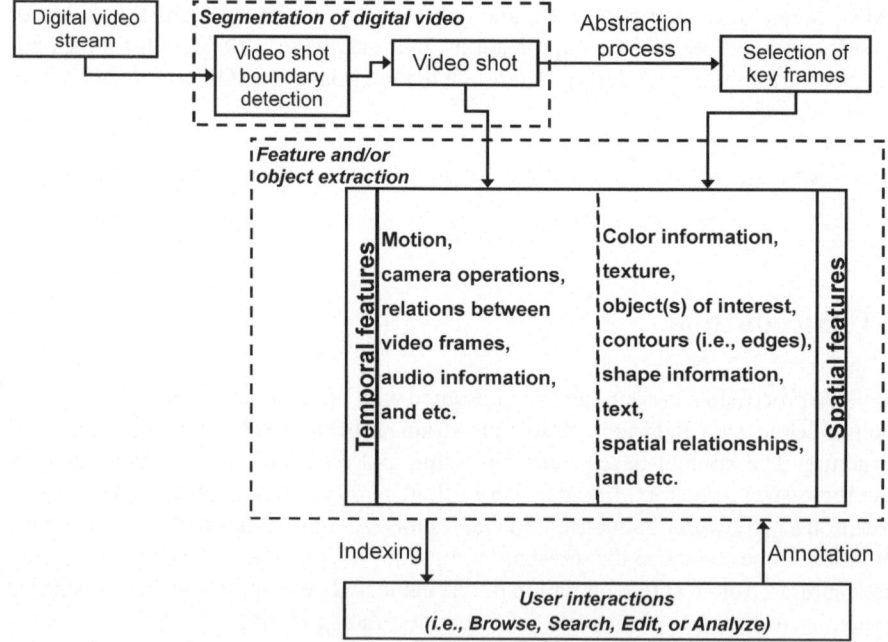

Fig. 2.1 The schematic for content-based retrieval of video databases

Human and computer vision work similar in terms of functionality, but have not exactly same functions and results [57, 58]. In this frame, the essentials of visual surveillance systems based on the basic elements should be considered. A camera is a device that records and stores (still) images from a given scene, also it is the basic sensing element [57]. Usually, the camera operations explicitly reflects how the attention of the viewer (i.e., human) should be directed [56]. Sensing with camera is the first step for a object D&T process of a visual surveillance system. A movie or video (i.e., captured by a camera) continuously takes some video frames per second as long as the user's choices (i.e., the length of the video). Generally, digital signal and image processing are the essential parts or levels for digital video processing. The object detection process affects on the object tracking and classification processes in video-content analysis, and video information retrieval via digital video processing [57].

In object D&T applications, manual D&T of object(s) is a tedious and exhausting task. Therefore, the experts in computer vision area studied for long periods of time on semiautomatic and automatic D&T techniques. These D&T techniques often involve maintaining a model, which is related to the spatial relationship between the various features [59]. In the literature, some image features, such as color, shape, texture, contours (e.g., edges), and motion (i.e., trajectory and spatial relationship) can be used to track the moving object(s) in videos. One can see that these features are given as spatial features in Fig. 2.1.

Video segmentation has two major types which are spatial and temporal segmentation. The spatial segmentation is based on the approach of digital image segmentation. Also, the temporal segmentation is constructed by time-based, meaningful, and manageable segments (i.e., video shots) in videos. According to Koprinska and Carrato [56], the temporal video segmentation is the first step toward automatic annotation of digital video sequences, and thus, its goal is to divide the video stream into a set of video shots that are used as basic elements for indexing. Therefore, each video shot is then represented by selecting key frames and indexed by extracting spatial and temporal features. The video retrieval process is based on the similarity between feature vector of the query and already stored video features [56].

Digital image segmentation is generally used to partition an image as bi-level or higher level into different regions that they belong to given image or video frame. This partition process can be either locally or globally. Semiautomatic image segmentation involves end-user interactions to separate the interested object(s) from background that the object is involved by the region of interest (ROI). Automatic image segmentation is similar to semiautomatic one, but it aims to separate and identify the object(s) in given ROI or in whole image that it works without end-user's intervention. The identification is based on the accurate boundaries of the object(s).

Tracking of a moving object over time is a challenging issue on video processing. The researchers developed a lot of video processing software to detect the position of an object in each image (i.e., video frame) in given sequence, and hence a temporal sequence of coordinates is determined [60]. If one realize this process for each image in given sequence and simply concatenate the positions of given object, thus the tracking is often considered as successfully accomplished. According to the textbook of Moeslund [60], the above mentioned approach, however, not considered tracking since each detection is done independently of all other detections. The main reason is that there is no temporal information in tracking process. The points in a coordinate system that are traveled by an object in a time scale are considered as the trajectory of this moving object. This approach can be extended to the states of object. These states are often stored in a state vector, where each entry in this vector contains the value of a certain parameter at a particular time [60]. Therefore, a general form of a moving object tracking process turns into an update process of previous states. The entries of state vector could be some features, such as position, velocity, acceleration, size, shape, color, texture and etc.

According to the study of Liu et al. [4], in distribution-based object D&T approach, Background Subtraction (BS) is the most popular method to detect moving object(s). The main idea of this approach is to estimate an appropriate representation (i.e., background image model) of the given scene based on pixel distribution. Also, the object(s) in the current video frame can be detected by subtracting the current video frame with the background model.

In addition, Liu et al. [4] expressed that the Optical Flow (OF) is the most widely used method in orientation-based object D&T approach. The OF approach approximates the moving object motion by estimating vectors originating or terminating at pixels in image (i.e., video frame) sequences. Also, the velocity field is represented by OF, which warps one image into another high dimensional feature space. The motion detection methods based on OF can accurately detect motion in the direction of intensity gradient [9, 10]. However, Liu et al. [4] drew attention to issue of motion that the motion is tangential to the intensity gradient cannot be well represented by the feature map. Furthermore, the illumination changes affect badly on OF-based methods.

The contour-based object D&T approaches also are not covered in our study. The main reason is that these methods cannot handle fast moving object very well, also they are computationally expensive and insensitive to illumination changes [4, 6–8].

The approaches based on the color probability distribution or color-clustering deal often with dynamical changes of color probability distribution (CPD). In this frame, in order to track colored object(s) in given video frame sequence, the color image data has to be represented as a probability distribution [57]. Generally, color distributions derived from video frame sequences change over time, also the object D&T method has to be modified to adopt dynamically to the probability distribution. Therefore, such methods use color histograms to track moving object(s). A good example to this approach is CAMShift tracker that it is based on MS color clustering approach. This color clustering (i.e., spatial segmentation) is also based on MS filtering (MSF) procedure that is a straightforward extension of the discontinuity preserving smoothing algorithm [36, 57]. This kind of object D&T process has lower computation cost than the approaches based on graph-cut or active contour models as well.

In our study, detailed information is given in Sect. 2.2 for background subtraction (BS) method, in Sect. 2.3 for Mean-shift (MS), Mean-shift filtering (MSF) and continuously adaptive Mean-shift (CMS or CAMShift) methods, in Sect. 2.4 for optical flow (OF) method and its variants as Horn–Schunck (HS) (i.e., Dense OF) and Lucas–Kanade (LK) (i.e., Sparse OF) techniques in this book, respectively. These methods are used for both of object D&T steps in our ViCamPEv software.

2.2 Background Subtraction

The detection of interesting foreground object from a video sequence provides a classification of the pixels into either foreground or background [61]. A scene in object detection process can be usually represented with a model called background model. The related algorithm (or method) finds deviations from the model for each incoming frame. Note that, the former form of this method is called sometimes frame differencing. This process is usually referred as the background subtraction [17, 30]. When the scene is stationary or gradually evolving, then the foreground detection can be solved conveniently with many traditional BS algorithms [61]. The statistical modeling techniques [12] and their variants [13] are often used in the literature [61]. The performance of these methods or techniques deteriorates when the scene involves dynamic elements or occluded fronts, such as waving trees, flocks of birds, rippling water, fog, or smoke, etc.

Common BS techniques were reviewed in Benezeth et al. study [62]. According to Benezeth et al. [62], the principle of BS methods can be summarized by the following rule,

$$\lambda_t(s) = \begin{cases} 1, & \text{if } m(I_{s,t}, B_s) > \tau_H \\ 0, & \text{otherwise} \end{cases} \tag{2.1}$$

where λ_t is the motion label field at time t and a function of $s(x, y)$ spatial location (also called motion mask), m is a distance between $I_{s,t}$ the video frame at time t at pixel s and B_s the background at pixel s; and τ_H is a threshold. The main differences between most BS methods are how well B_s is modeled and which distance metric m is being used (e.g., Euclidean, Manhattan, Mahalanobis, and etc.) [17, 62]. There are four main steps in a BS algorithm which are explained in Cheung and Kamath's study [63], namely the preprocessing, background modeling, foreground detection, and data validation. According to Cheung and Kamath's study [63], preprocessing step involves some simple image processing tasks, which change the raw input video sequence into a format that is used in subsequent steps. In background modeling step, the new video frame can be used in the calculation and updating process of a background model. This model provides a statistical description of the entire background scene. This scene may be static or dynamic [57]. In the foreground detection step, some pixels in given video frame, which are not explained enough by given background model [32], are defined as a binary candidate foreground mask [57, 63].

In this frame, the background modeling techniques can be classified into two broad categories: nonrecursive and recursive techniques. For nonrecursive techniques, representative work includes frame differencing, median filter, linear predictive filter, and nonparametric model. A nonrecursive technique uses a sliding-window approach for background estimation. This approach stores a buffer of the previous video frames. Therefore, it estimates the background image based on the temporal variation of each pixel within the buffer. These techniques are highly adaptive as they do not depend on the history beyond those frames stored in the buffer [63]. The recursive techniques are frequently based on the approximated median filter, Kalman filter, and mixture of Gaussian (MoG) [57]. Recursive techniques do not maintain a buffer for background estimation. Also, they recursively update a single background model based on each input video frame. As a result, input frames from distant past could have an effect on the current background model. According to the study of Cheung and Kamath [63], compared with nonrecursive techniques, the recursive techniques require less storage. In addition, any error in the background model of these techniques can linger for a much longer period of time. In Fig. 2.2, the schematic for a general object D&T system based on the recursive BS is shown.

In Fig. 2.2, there are five steps: preprocessing, BS with updating, foreground detection, post-processing, and tracking with foreground mask. The preprocessing and BS with updating (i.e., background modeling) steps are similar to the steps which are explained in Cheung and Kamath's study [63]. In post-processing step, some corrections are made on given binary image via connected component analysis (CCA), and etc. In tracking with foreground mask step (i.e., Step V in Fig. 2.2), the tracking process is achieved by spatio-temporal information about moving object. At decision point between Step IV and Step V in Fig. 2.2, the algorithm that works on underlying system looks up the spatial and temporal coherency for moving object; if given object is labeled as stationary in a certain number of video frames, then this object will be embedded in the background model as a part of the model, and the background model can be updated immediately with this new information. However,

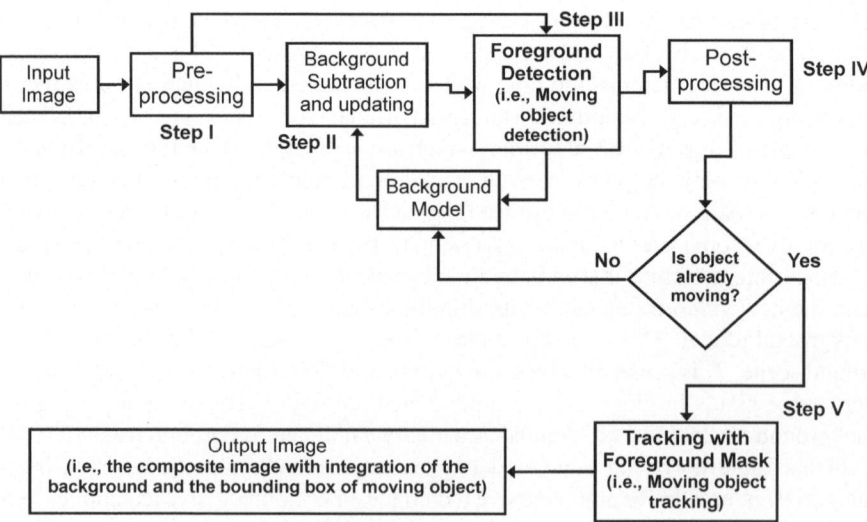

Fig. 2.2 The schematic for a general object D&T system based on the recursive BS

if the object is already moveable, then it is tracked as a foreground mask. This foreground mask is frequently a binary image (i.e., black and white image) and also its white regions are usually treated as the moving objects by BS algorithm.

In the literature, many approaches for automatically adapting a background model to dynamic scene variations are proposed. Detailed information for the aforementioned techniques can be found in the literature [30, 62, 63] as well. Some implementations of recursive BS are used in our ViCamPEv software.

2.2.1 Literature Review

For foreground detection in dynamic scenes, there are two main categories of relevant approaches, namely pixel level and region level [61]. In the pixel-level models, the scene model has a probability density function (PDF) for each pixel separately. According to Zivkovic and van der Heijden [13], a pixel from a new image is considered to be a background pixel, if its new value is well described by its density function. The simplest mode is often given for a static scene that it could be just an image of the scene without the intruding objects [13]. Furthermore, the variances of the pixel intensity levels from the image can vary from pixel to pixel. In the study of Mittal and Paragios [11], they used an elaborated adaptive kernel density estimation scheme to build a nonparametric model of color and optical flow (OF) at each pixel. According to Wu and Peng's study [61], when the same motions are observed many times in a certain number of frames, then the method of Mittal and Paragios [11] provides good detection results. The nonparametric density estimates also lead to flexible models. In addition, the kernel density estimate was proposed for BS in the literature [15], but there is a problem with kernel estimates that the choice of the kernel size is considered as fixed. This problem can be overcome by the use of variable-size kernels [64]. In the study of Wang and Suter [65], they presented a concept named 'sample consensus'. This concept defined how many times the current pixel agreed with previous samples at that pixel site, and thus, the foreground and background are separated by thresholding each consensus value.

On the other hand, the region-level methods are based on the relationship between pixels. In the study of Sheikh and Shah [66], they proposed a kernel density estimation to model the full background as a single distribution. In their study, the pixel locations were unified into the distribution, eliminating one distribution per pixel. Their experimental results show that the appealing performance of Sheikh and Shah's method. In the study of Zhong and Sclaroff [67], an autoregressive moving average model was employed to model the dynamic textured background, and exploited a robust Kalman filter to estimate the intrinsic appearance of dynamic texture as well as the foreground regions. In addition, Dalley et al. [68] introduced a generalization of the MoG model to handle dynamic textures. According to the study of Wu and Peng [61], they treated the image generation process as arising from a mixture of components consisting of a Gaussian distribution in color and some spatial distribution. Experiments validated the correctness and effectiveness of their algorithm [68].

In the literature, there are a lot of studies that they issued some variants of BS method. Mandellos et al. [69] presented an innovative system for detecting and extracting vehicles in traffic surveillance scenes. Their system covers locating moving objects present in complex road scenes by implementing an advanced BS methodology. In their study, a histogram-based filtering procedure was concerned by the innovation that this procedure collects scatter background information carried in a series of frames, at pixel level, generating reliable instances of the actual background. A background instance on demand under any traffic conditions was reconstructed by the proposed algorithm. According to Mandellos et al. study [69], the background reconstruction algorithm demonstrated a rather robust performance in various operating conditions including unstable lighting, different view-angles, and congestion.

In the study of Spagnolo et al. [70], they addressed the problem of moving object segmentation using BS. They proposed a reliable foreground segmentation algorithm that combines temporal image analysis with a reference background image. In their study, a new approach for background adaptation to changes in illumination was presented. All the pixels in the image, even those covered by foreground objects that they are continuously updated in the background model. The experimental results of their study demonstrated the effectiveness of the proposed algorithm when applied in different outdoor and indoor environments.

In the study of Zhang and Ding [71], a tracking algorithm based on adaptive BS about the video D&T moving objects was presented. In first stage, they used a median filter to achieve the background image of the video and denoise the sequence of video. In second stage, they used adaptive BS algorithm to detect and track the moving objects. Adaptive background updating was also realized by the study of Zhang and Ding [71], finally, they improved the accuracy of tracking through open operation. The simulation results of their study show that the adaptive BS is useful in both D&T moving objects, and BS algorithm runs more quickly.

In the study of Shoushtarian and Bez [72], they presented and compared three dynamic BS algorithm for color images. The performances of these algorithms defined as 'Selective Update using Temporal Averaging', 'Selective Update using Non-foreground Pixels of the Input Image', and 'Selective Update using Temporal Median' are only different for background pixels. Then, they used an invariant color filter and a suitable motion tracking technique, an object-level classification was also offered that recognizes the behaviors of all foreground blobs. Their approach, which selectively excludes foreground blobs from the background frames, was included in all three methods. They showed that the 'Selective Update using Temporal Median' produces the correct background image for each input frame. The third algorithm operates in unconstrained outdoor and indoor scenes. Also, the efficiency of the new algorithm was confirmed by the results obtained on a number of image sequences.

In the study of Magee [73], a vehicle tracking algorithm was presented based on the combination of a novel per-pixel background model and a set of foreground models of object size, position, velocity, and color distribution. The background model is based on the Gaussian mixture (GM). According to study of Magee [73], each pixel in the scene was explained as either background, belonging to a foreground object, or as noise. A projective ground-plane transform was used within the foreground model to strengthen object size and velocity consistency assumptions. In the study, a learned model of typical road travel direction and speed was used to provide a prior estimate of object velocity, which is used to initialize the velocity model for each of the foreground objects. In the experimental results, their system was worked at near video frame rate (i.e., greater than 20 fps) on modest hardware and is robust assuming sufficient image resolution is available and vehicle sizes do not greatly exceed the priors on object size used in object initialization.

In El Maadi and Maldague's study [74], a framework was proposed to detect, track, and classify both pedestrians and vehicles in realistic scenarios using a stationary infrared camera. In addition, a novel dynamic BS technique to robustly adapt detection to illumination changes in outdoor scenes was proposed. Their experimental results show that combining results with edge detection enables to reduce considerably false alarms (FA) while this reinforces also tracking efficiency. El Maadi and Maldague declared that their proposed system was implemented and tested successfully in various environmental conditions.

In Davis and Sharma's study [75], they presented a new BS technique fusing contours from thermal and visible imagery for persistent object detection in urban settings. Statistical BS in the thermal domain was used to identify the initial ROI. Also, color and intensity information were used within these areas to obtain the corresponding ROIs in the visible domain. Within each region, input and background gradient information were combined to form a contour saliency map (CSM). The binary contour fragments were obtained from corresponding CSMs that they are then fused into a single image. In their study, an A^* path-constrained search (i.e., a search algorithm that is widely used in pathfinding and graph traversal) along watershed boundaries of the ROIs was used to complete and close any broken segments in the fused contour image. At the end, the contour image was flood-filled to produce silhouettes. The results of their approach were evaluated quantitatively and compared with other low- and high-level fusion techniques using manually segmented data.

2.3 Mean-Shift and Continuously Adaptive Mean-Shift

In the literature, Mean-shift (MS) approach is a clustering approach in image segmentation. MS was originally proposed by Comaniciu and Meer [76] to find clusters in the joint spatial-color space. In the literature, MS algorithm is detailed in some studies [17, 30, 36, 76–79]. MS is susceptible to fall into local maxima in case of clutter or occlusion [79]. Nummiaro et al. [80] declared that MS-based trackers easily fail in tracking rapid moving objects. They cannot recover from the possible failures. Furthermore, these trackers' efficiency is important against robustness. In addition, they cannot deal with multimodal (i.e., for scenes with multiobject) problems [17, 81, 82]. Continuously adaptive Mean-shift (CMS or CAMShift) is a tracking method. CMS is a modified form of MS method. In CMS, MS algorithm is modified to deal with dynamically changing color probability distributions (CPDs) derived from video frame sequences. Color histograms were used in Bradski's study [34] via new algorithm is called CMS. In a single image (or in a single frame of a video sequence), the CMS process is iterated until convergence criterion is met [17]. When the tracked object's color does not change, the MS-based CMS trackers are quite robust. However, if similar colors appear in the background, then MS-based CMS trackers easily fail in tracking. The Coupled CMS algorithm was demonstrated in a real-time head tracking application [34, 35]. The algorithm of a general CMS tracker is used as a part of Open Source Computer Vision library (OpenCV) [77, 78]. Furthermore, the CMS tracker tracks usually a specified object, which is defined or detected by system [17]. Similar implementation of CMS tracker is used in our ViCamPEv software.

2.3.1 Mean-Shift and Mean-Shift Filtering

The segmentation procedure based on the Mean-shift (MS) analysis is used to analyze complex multimodal feature space and identification of feature clusters. This procedure is iterative and used to seek the mode of a density function presented by local samples. Furthermore, its approach is called nonparametric, because a complete density is being modeled [17, 36, 78, 83, 84]. The MS clustering is a method to cluster an image by associating each pixel with a peak of the image's probability density, and also, it is provided that this procedure is a quadratic bound maximization both for stationary and evolving sample sets [85]. For MS clustering, its ROI size and shape parameters are only free parameters on MS process, i.e., the multivariate density kernel estimator [57].

The MS algorithm is initialized with a large number of hypothesized cluster centers randomly chosen from the data of the given image. The algorithm aims at finding of nearest stationary point of underlying density function of data [30]. The peak in the local density is computed by first defining a window in the neighborhood of the pixel. Also, its utility is that the detecting the modes of the density is easy by using MS process. Therefore, the mean of the pixel that lie within the window can be calculated. This window is then shifted to the mean [86]. For this purpose, each cluster center is moved to the mean of the data lying inside the multidimensional window centered on the cluster center [30]. Until convergence, the similar steps are repeated. The outcome of the MS process is only controlled by the kernel size (i.e., bandwidth). Thence, MS requires less manual intervention compared to other clustering algorithms. However, too large or small bandwidth may lead under- or over-segmentation problems. Zhou et al. [86] discussed about the integration of different algorithms with MS in order to find an optimal solution that this integration is used to effectively handle segmentation problems. In MS clustering procedure, the algorithm builds up a vector that is defined by the old and the new cluster centers, which is called MS vector. It is computed iteratively until the cluster centers do not change their positions. Also, some cluster may get merged during the iterations of MS process [30, 36, 57, 76].

The mean-shift filtering (MSF) is based on a smooth continuous nonparametric model. In the literature, a well-known noniterative discontinuity preserving smoothing technique is the bilateral filtering (BF). According to Comaniciu and Meer's studies [36, 76], the use of local information [76] is the essential difference between the BF- and the MSF-based smoothing. In MSF, the spatial coordinates of each pixel are adjusted along with its color values (i.e., joint domain of color and location). This joint domain of color and location is based on $[l, u, v, x, y]$ space, where (l, u, v) represents the color and (x, y) represents the spatial location [30]. Therefore, the pixel migrates more quickly toward other pixels with similar colors. It can later be used for clustering and segmentation [83]. The image segmentation based on MSF procedure is a straightforward extension of the discontinuity preserving smoothing algorithm. In the process, each pixel associates with a significant mode of the joint domain density located in its neighborhood [76].

The MS vector is derived by estimating the density gradient that the vector always points toward the direction of maximum increase in density. The density modes in the feature space (i.e., local maxima) can thus be located by computing the MS vector [87]. In addition, the smoothing through replacing the pixel in the center of a window by the (weighted) average of the pixels in the window indiscriminately blurs the image [76]. However, it removes not only the noise, but also the salient information. The MS-based discontinuity preserving smoothing algorithm is called as the mean-shift filtering (MSF). Also, the information beyond the individual windows is taken into account in the image smoothed by MSF [76].

In the d-dimensional Euclidean space $\mathbf{R}^d$, given n data points $x_i, i = 1, 2, \ldots, n$, the kernel density estimator of point x with kernel $K(x)$ and bandwidth h is given by [76, 87]

$$\hat{f}_{h,K}(x) = \frac{1}{nh^d} \sum_{i=1}^{n} K\left(\frac{x - x_i}{h}\right). \tag{2.2}$$

In the mathematical background, the radially symmetric kernels are usually used which satisfy

$$K(x) = c_{k,d} k\left(\left\|x\right\|^2\right) \tag{2.3}$$

where $c_{k,d}$ is the normalization constant, and $k(x)$ is called the profile of the kernel [76, 87]. Also, $x \in \mathbf{R}^d$ is a point in the d-dimensional feature space, and $\|\cdot\|$ is a norm. The density estimator in Eq. (2.2) can be rewritten as [87]

$$\hat{f}_{h,K}(x) = \frac{c_{k,d}}{nh^d} \sum_{i=1}^{n} k\left(\left\|\frac{x - x_i}{h}\right\|^2\right). \tag{2.4}$$

According to Szeliski [83], starting at some guess for a local maximum, y_j, which can be a random input data point x_i, MS clustering computes the gradient of the density estimate $\hat{f}_{h,K}(x)$ at y_j and takes an uphill step in that direction [83]. This approach is a variant of multiple restart gradient descent. Therefore, the gradient of $\hat{f}_{h,K}(x)$ can be expressed as [76, 87]

$$\nabla \hat{f}_{h,K}(x) = \hat{f}_{h,Q}(x) \frac{2c_{k,d}}{h^2 c_{q,d}} m_{h,Q}(x) \tag{2.5}$$

where $q(x) - k'(x)$, and $k'(x)$ is the first derivative of $k(x)$. The Q is another kernel that its profile is q. In this frame, the MS vector $m_{h,Q}(x)$ can be expressed as [87]

$$m_{h,Q}(x) = \frac{\sum_{i=1}^{n} x_i q\left(\left\|\frac{x-x_i}{h}\right\|^2\right)}{\sum_{i=1}^{n} q\left(\left\|\frac{x-x_i}{h}\right\|^2\right)} - x. \tag{2.6}$$

As Szeliski [83] discussed in his textbook, the MS vector acts as the difference between the weighted mean of the neighbors x_i around x and the current value of x. The kernels are adjusted accordingly to location and color that they may have different scales. A multivariate normal kernel to be optimal one for the MS procedure that is given as [76]

$$K(x) = (2\pi)^{-d/2} \exp\left(-\frac{1}{2}\|x\|^2\right). \tag{2.7}$$

The Epanechnikov kernel is the shadow of the uniform kernel, i.e., the d-dimensional unit sphere, while the normal kernel and its shadow have the same expression [76]. The CMS trackers use MS segmentation that it is based on MSF.

Denote by $\{y_j\}_{j=1,2,...}$ the sequence of successive locations of the kernel Q. Let x_i and $z_i, i = 1, \ldots, n$, be the d-dimensional input and filtered image pixels in the joint spatial-range domain, respectively. This joint spatial-range domain $d[x_p, y_p, l, u, v]$ is a five dimensional vector, where (x_p, y_p) is the pixel location and (l, u, v) are the values of color components. Comaniciu and Meer [76] used the *CIE L*u*v** as the perceptually uniform color space. They employed *CIE L*u*v** motivated by a linear mapping property. In addition, there is no clear advantage between using *CIE L*u*v** or *CIE L*a*b** color space. The *CIE L*a*b** is a three-dimensional model that each color is treated as a point in a three-dimensional space, where the difference between two colors is based on the Euclidean distance. It has a color-opponent space with dimension L for lightness, and also, a and b for the color-opponent dimensions. In this context, the MSF procedure in Table 2.1 can be also applied to each pixel as given below [76, 87].

In Table 2.1, the superscripts s and r denote the spatial and range components of given vector, respectively. Comaniciu and Meer [76] discussed that the filtered data at the spatial location x_i^s will have the range component of the point of convergence $y_{i,c}^r$. At the end of the MS clustering (also MSF) process, all data points was visited by the MS procedure converging to the same mode, which forms a cluster of arbitrary shape [87].

Table 2.1 The MSF procedure from the study of Comaniciu and Meer [76]

Step 1.	Initialize $j = 1$ and $y_{i,1} = x_i$
Step 2.	Compute $y_{i,j+1}$,

$$y_{j+1} = y_j + m_{h,q} = \frac{\sum_{i=1}^{n} x_i q \left(\left\| \frac{y_j - x_i}{h} \right\|^2 \right)}{\sum_{i=1}^{n} q \left(\left\| \frac{y_j - x_i}{h} \right\|^2 \right)}, j = 1, 2, \ldots$$

until convergence, $y = y_{i,c}$,

Step 3.	Assign $z_i = \left(x_i^s, y_{i,c}^r \right)$

2.3.2 Continuously Adaptive Mean-Shift

The MS segmentation is based on the MSF procedure that it is based on MS clustering. The advantages of MS segmentation is its modularity that the control of segmentation output is very simple. Comaniciu and Meer [76] introduced the basis of MS segmentation in their study that x_i and z_i, $i = 1, 2, \ldots, n$, are given as the d-dimensional input and filtered image pixels in the joint spatial-range domain and Ψ_i as the label of the ith pixel in the segmented image, respectively. Therefore, the MS segmentation procedure in Table 2.2 can be also applied to each pixel [76, 87].

The essential idea is that an initial window (i.e., kernel) is placed over a two-dimensional array of data points and is successively recentered over the mode (or local peak) of its data distribution until convergence [77]. As mentioned before, the CMS or CAMShift is a tracking method that is a modified form of MS method. The MS algorithm operates on color probability distributions (CPDs), and CMS is a modified form of MS to deal with dynamical changes of CPDs [57]. In the literature, some color spaces were used to detect and track the moving object(s). In color image segmentation or color clustering, the most significant point is how to measure the difference between two or more colors. Also, *RGB* stands for Red (*R*), Green (*G*), and Blue (*B*) colors. The *HSV* stands for Hue (*H*), Saturation (*S*), and Value (*V*). In addition, *HSV* has an alternative name as *HSL/I* that it has hue, saturation, and

Table 2.2 The MS segmentation procedure from the study of Comaniciu and Meer [76]

Step 1.	Run the MSF procedure for the image and store all the information about d-dimensional convergence point in z_i, $z_i = y_{i,c}$,
Step 2.	Delineate in the joint domain the clusters $\{C_p\}_{p=1,2,\ldots,m}$ by grouping together all z_i, which are closer than h_s, in the spatial domain and h_r in the range domain, by this way, the basins of attraction of the corresponding convergence points are concatenated.
Step 3.	For each $i = 1, \ldots, n$, assign $\Psi_i = \{p \mid z_i \in C_p\}$.
Step 4.	As an optional choice: Eliminate spatial regions containing less than M pixels.

lightness/intensity components. The *HSV* is a most common cylindrical-coordinate representation of points, which are given in a *RGB* color space model.

In the literature, the *HSV* color space is used to segment, detect, and track the moving object by CMS trackers. To track colored objects in video frame sequences, the color image data has to be represented as a probability distribution [34, 35, 57]. The main reason is that the computational complexity of *HSV* is lower than *CIE L*a*b** color space. In addition, the *HSV* color space has a better quantization than *CIE L*a*b** color space, and also, the better quantization is to cause a better segmentation, but the *HSV* color space has a worse computational complexity than *RGB* color space. Kerminen and Gabbouj [88] compared three different color spaces with each other, which are *RGB*, *HSV*, and *CIE L*a*b** color spaces. The reader may refer for detailed information to the study of Kerminen and Gabbouj [88].

To accomplish the tracking moving object, Bradski used color histograms in his study [34, 57]. Color distributions derived from video image sequences change over time, so the MS algorithm has to be modified to adapt dynamically to the probability distribution it is tracking. The novel algorithm in Bradski's study (i.e., CMS) meets all these requirements. In a single image, the CMS (or CAMShift) process is iterated until convergence or until an upper bound on the number of iterations is reached. When the tracked target object's color does not change, the MS-based CMS trackers are quite robust and stable. However, they are easily distracted when similar colors appear in the background.

The Coupled CMS algorithm (as given in the study of Bradski [34]) is demonstrated in a real-time head tracking application that it is a part of the Intel OpenCV Computer Vision library [77, 78]. The Coupled CMS is reviewed in François's study [35] as well. The reader may refer to the reference [34] and [35] for some implementations of the algorithm in face tracking. In addition, the face tracking is used to control various interactive programs via head movements [57]. The head's color model is actually a skin color tone model in *HSI* (i.e., *HSV*) color space. The Hue component of *HSI* for color images gives relatively best results for skin color tone-based tracking. A universal framework for the distributed implementation of algorithms called software architecture for *immersipresence* is used by François [35] as well.

A system design involving a CAMShift tracker is presented by François [35] as a black-box approach based on the CAMShift tracker via an instance of *CvCamShift-Tracker* class of OpenCV library. In addition, OpenCV and the software architecture for *immersipresence* are used to design and implement a CAMShift-based tracking system in the study of François [35]. For better understanding, an exemplary depiction of the design is given in Fig. 2.3 in which OpenCV's CAMShift tracker [57, 77, 78] is taken as basis for the design of general object D&T system based on a CAMShift tracker.

In Fig. 2.3, an input image (or the first frame of given video) in *RGB* color space is converted at Step I to *HSV* color space. Then, the histogram computation according to backprojection can be calculated in Step II. Also, in Step III, CAMShift tracker identifies the moving object and describes the new bounding box properties for object D&T such as box size and orientation. Thus, the last known bounding box can be updated by using this way. This is an iterative procedure. In Step IV, the set of

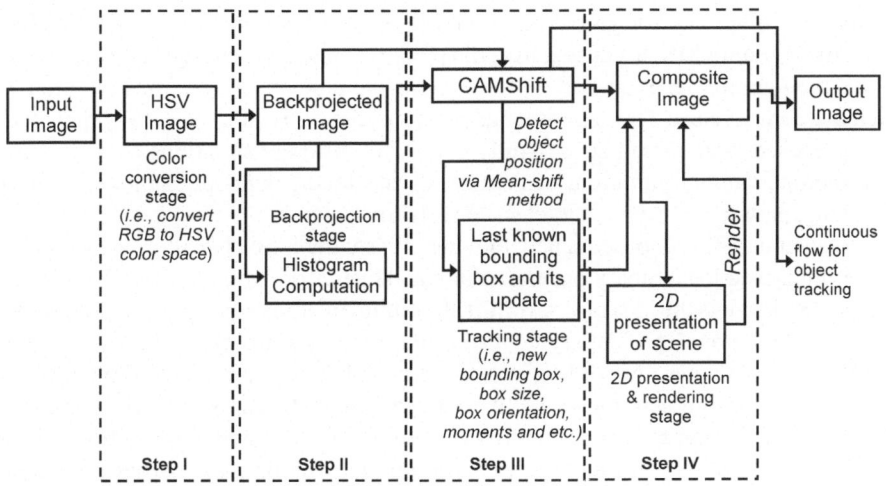

Fig. 2.3 The schematic for a general object D&T system based on a CAMShift tracker (figure adapted from the study of Karasulu [57])

bounding box, detected boundaries and segmented object are merged together on to original background image and rendered as a composite image (i.e., rendering using 2-*Dimensional* scene information). The output image (or video frame) is based on this composite image, meanwhile, the flow of tracking for CAMShift continues until the video is finished.

2.3.3 Literature Review

In the literature, there are numerous studies related to the MS-based CMS (or CAMShift) trackers. In the study of Stern and Efros [89], they developed a procedure that adaptively switches color space models throughout the processing of a video. Also, they proposed a new performance measure for evaluating tracking algorithm. Their proposed methodology is used to find the optimal color space and color distribution models combination in the design of adaptive color tracking systems. Their color switching procedure was performed inside the framework of the CAMShift tracking algorithm. They combined a number of procedures to construct an enriched face tracking approach. At each iteration of the CAMShift algorithm, given image is converted into a probability image using the model of color distribution of the skin color being tracked. In the study of Li et al. [90], they proposed a novel approach for global target tracking based on MS technique. The proposed method represents the model and the candidate in terms of background- and color-weighted histogram, respectively, which can obtain precise object size adaptively with low computational complexity. Also, they implemented the MS procedure via a coarse-to-fine way for global maximum seeking. This procedure was termed as adaptive pyramid MS, because it uses the pyramid analysis technique and can determine the pyramid level adaptively to decrease the number of iterations required to achieve convergence. The experimental results of the study of Li et al. [90] show that the proposed method can successfully cope with different situations such as camera motion, camera vibration, camera zoom and focus, high-speed moving object tracking, partial occlusions, target scale variations, etc.

Yuan et al. [91] proposed a new moving objects tracking algorithm, which combines improved local binary pattern texture and hue information to describe moving objects and adopts the idea of CAMShift algorithm. In order to reduce matching complexity on the premise of satisfying the accuracy, many kinds of local binary pattern and hue are cut down. According to Yuan et al. [91], the experiments show that the proposed algorithm can track effectively moving objects, can satisfy real-time and has better performance than others. In the study of Mazinan and Amir-Latifi [92], an improved convex kernel function was proposed to overcome the partial occlusion. Therefore, in order to improve the MS algorithm against the low saturation and also sudden light, changes are made from motion information of the desired sequence. By using both the color feature and the motion information simultaneously, the capability of the MS algorithm was correspondingly increased. In their study [92], by assuming a constant speed for the object, a robust estimator, i.e., the Kalman filter, was realized to solve the full occlusion problem. According to Mazinan and Amir-Latifi [92], the experimental results verified that the proposed method has an optimum performance in real-time object tracking, while the result of the original MS algorithm may be unsatisfied.

Jung and Han [93] proposed a hybrid approach of the two methods for text localization in complex images. An automatically constructed the texture classifier based on multilayer perceptron (MLP) can increase the recall rates for complex images with much less user intervention and no explicit feature extraction. The connected component-based filtering based on the geometry and shape information enhances the precision rates without affecting overall performance. Afterward, the time-consuming texture analysis for less relevant pixels was avoided by using CAMShift. According to Jung and Han [93], the experimental results show that the proposed hybrid approach leads to not only robust but also efficient text localization. In the study of Babu et al. [94], they presented a novel online adaptive object tracker based on fast learning radial basis function (RBF) networks. They have compared the proposed tracker against the MS tracker, which is known for robust object tracking in cluttered environment. Also, the pixel-based color features were used for developing the target object model in their study. In addition, two separate RBF networks were used, one of which is trained to maximize the classification accuracy of object pixels, while the other is trained for non-object pixels. The target was modeled using the posterior probability of object and non-object classes. Object localization was achieved by iteratively seeking the mode of the posterior probability of the pixels in each of the subsequent frames. Therefore, an adaptive learning procedure was presented to update the object model in order to tackle object appearance and illumination changes. According to Babu et al. [94], the superior performance of the proposed tracker is illustrated with many complex video sequences, as compared against the popular color-based MS tracker. Therefore, the proposed tracker is suitable for real-time object tracking due to its low computational complexity.

Wang et al. [95] proposed a novel algorithm for tracking object in video sequence that it is called as CAMShift guided particle filter (CAMSGPF). CAMShift was incorporated into the probabilistic framework of particle filter (PF) as an optimization scheme for proposal distribution. CAMShift helps improve the sampling efficiency of particle filter in both position and scale space, also, it achieves better scale adaptation and can be applied in a simplified way without much loss in performance. According to Wang et al. [95], the CAMSGPF outperforms standard particle filter and MS embedded particle filter (MSEPF) based trackers in terms of both robustness and efficiency. Yin et al. [96] proposed an algorithm that combines CAMShift with PF using multiple cues. The effectiveness of particles was improved and the tracking window can change scale with the target adaptively because of the use of CAMShift. Meanwhile, an adaptive integration method was used to combine color information with motion information. Therefore, the problems can be solved with this way which are encountered in tracking an object with illumination variation and the background color clutter. In addition, an occlusion handler was proposed by Yin et al. [96] to handle the full occlusion for a long time.

In the study of González-Ortega et al. [97], a marker-free computer vision system for cognitive rehabilitation tests monitoring was presented. Their system monitors and analyzes the correct and incorrect realization of a set of psychomotricity exercises in which a hand has to touch a facial feature. Different human body parts were used D&T in this monitoring. Detection of eyes, nose, face, and hands was achieved with a set of classifiers built independently based on the AdaBoost algorithm. In their study, comparisons with other detection approaches, regarding performance, and applicability to the monitoring system were presented. Also, face and hands tracking was accomplished through the CAMShift algorithm. González-Ortega et al. [97] described the CAMShift algorithm that it is an adaptation of MS, which uses continuously adaptive probability distributions, i.e., distributions that can be recomputed for each frame, and with a search windows size adaptation. Also, they declared that CAMShift needs structural features of the tracking object, and it is robust to temporal variations of the features [34, 97]. In their study, the CAMShift algorithm was applied with independent and adaptive two-dimensional histograms of the chromaticity components of the *TSL* color space for the pixels inside these three regions. In *TSL* color space, a color is specified in terms of Tint (T), Saturation (S), and Luminance (L) values. It has the advantage of extracting a given color robustly while minimizing illumination influence. In their study, the *TSL* color space was selected after a study of five color spaces regarding skin color characterization. According to González-Ortega et al. [97], the experimental results show that their monitoring system was achieved a successful monitoring percentage.

Hu et al. [98] presented an enhanced MS tracking algorithm using joint spatial-color feature and a novel similarity measure function. The target image was modeled with the kernel density estimation and new similarity measure functions were developed using the expectation of the estimated kernel density. Also, two similarity-based MS tracking algorithms were derived with these new similarity measure functions. In addition, the weighted-background information was added into the proposed tracking algorithm to enhance the robustness. The principal components of variance matrix were computed to update the orientation of the tracking object. The corresponding eigenvalues were used to monitor the scale of the object. According to Hu et al. [98], the experimental results show that the new similarity-based tracking algorithms can be implemented in real-time and are able to track the moving object with an automatic update of the orientation and scale changes.

2.4 Optical Flow

An optical flow (OF) is based on the idea that the brightness continuous for most points in the image [30, 57, 99], because of almost the same brightness is appeared on the neighboring points. The continuity equation for the optical term is given below [99],

$$\frac{\partial b}{\partial t} + v \nabla b = 0 \tag{2.8}$$

where v is the velocity vector and b is the brightness function. In addition, one can directly determine one-dimensional velocity in one-dimensional case, which is provided that the spatial derivative does not vanish. Also, the brightness is continuous. In the scope of aperture problems and scenes under varying illumination conditions, given 2D motion and apparent motion are not equivalent [17, 77, 100]. The OF methods are used for generating dense flow fields by computing the flow vector of each pixel under the brightness constancy constraint [30], its computation is detailed in the literature [101–103]. Extending OF methods to compute the translation of a rectangular region is trivial. Shi and Tomasi [104] proposed the KLT (Kanade-Lucas-Tomasi) feature tracker. In 'Good Features to Track' study of Shi and Tomasi [104], KLT tracker's basics are firstly presented. The corner detection algorithm of Shi and Tomasi is used in other image and video processing studies as well. In survey study of Yilmaz et al. [30], they talked about a translation equation which is similar to construction of the OF method proposed by Lucas and Kanade [102]. According to Shi and Tomasi [104], regardless of the method used for tracking, not all parts of an image contain complete motion information. This is known as aperture problem. For better understanding, for instance, only the vertical component of motion can be determined for a horizontal image intensity edge. The researchers have proposed to track corners to overcome this difficulty, or windows with a high spatial frequency content, or regions [104]. Note that, the corner point is a conjunction of two crossed line in given image, which is the essential part of the image intensity edge. In object D&T process, the image intensity edge(s) is generally used to determine the boundaries of the object(s) that this determination aims to segment the image as region-level or edge-level. In the Fig. 2.4, a schematic for a general object D&T system based on an OF tracker.

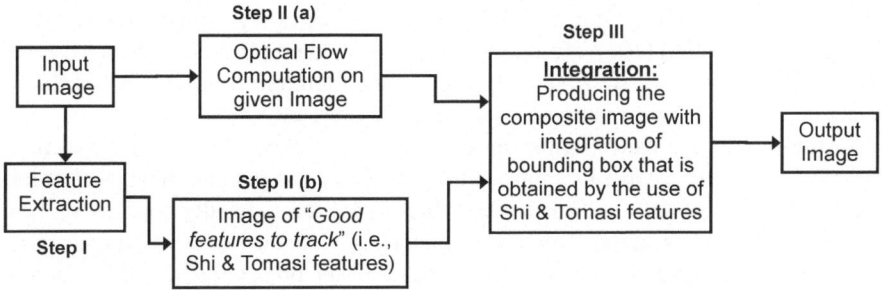

Fig. 2.4   The schematic for a general object D&T system based on an optical flow tracker

In Fig. 2.4, the Shi and Tomasi-based OF tracker takes an input image (or a frame of given video) at Step I, and then, the salient and significant features are extracted from given image. In Step II, there are two substep for OF computation and tracking. In Step II(a), the OF is computed on given current image (e.g., subsequent frame of given video, or an image other than first image), which is obtained from the flow between previous image (i.e., anchor frame of video) and given current image (i.e., target frame of video). This computation aims to show the direction of movement of moving parts based on the image velocity field. Also, in D&T process at Step II(b), the '*Good features to track*' image is constructed only by using selected features which are optimally chosen due to Shi and Tomasi technique. Generally, the selected features indicates the OF-based corner points of tracked object(s). In Step III, the bounding box (or boxes) of target object(s) is integrated with given image (or a frame of given video) to construct the composite image. This bounding box (or boxes) is obtained by using the set of Shi and Tomasi feature points which indicated the moving object(s) in sequence of successive images (or video frames). All feature points are extracted in Step I, and then, some of them are defined as '*Good features*' (i.e., optimally selected features) for given image in Step II (b). At the end, all integrations on the frame are shown on the output image, which involves bounding box (or boxes) for points of good features (i.e., corner points) for tracked object(s).

In the literature, the OF is a pixel-level representation model for motion patterns, in which each point in the image is assigned a motion vector, and, it is also known as a motion vector field [105]. Moreover, the techniques for estimating OF can be classified into three major categories, which are the phase correlation, block-based methods, and gradient-based estimation, respectively. Zheng and Xue [105] described these three categories in their study. According to their study, the phase correlation is a fast frequency-domain approach to estimating the relative movement between two images. Therefore, the block-based methods minimize the sum of squared differences or the sum of absolute differences, or maximize the normalized cross-correlation. It has been frequently used in video compression standards. Moreover, the gradient-based estimation is a function of the partial derivatives of the image signal and/or the desired flow field and higher order partial derivatives. In addition, the well-known

OF methods are belong to the aforementioned third category, which are the Lucas–Kanade (LK) method [102], Horn–Schunck (HS) method [101], Black–Jepson (BJ) method [106], and they are frequently used in the literature. By the way, we do not select the Black–Jepson method to implement in our study.

In this frame, we can consider in all aspects that there are two different main techniques for OF: Sparse OF and Dense OF. The most popular sparse OF tracking technique is the Lucas–Kanade OF, which is treated as locally constant motion. This method also has an implementation on OpenCV that it works with image pyramids, and allowing us to track the motions of faster objects [17]. This technique is referred as *Sparse OF* in our study. Another popular OF technique is a dense technique: the Horn–Schunck OF technique, which is treated as globally constant motion. This technique is referred as *Dense OF* in our study. Consequently, both kinds of implementations of OF tracker are used in our ViCamPEv software.

2.4.1 Horn–Schunck Technique (Dense OF)

The gradient-based methods are primarily based on the image flow constraint equation, which is derived from the brightness constancy assumption as well as the first-order Taylor series approximation [101, 107]. When one used only the image flow constraint equation alone, it is insufficient to compute the OF, because each equation involves two different variables. Also, a regularization approach is introduced by Horn and Schunck [101] that it employed a first order smoothness assumption to constrain the flow field and solve the flow [107]. According to the study of Teng et al. [108], the unsatisfactory performance of Horn and Schunck's regularization method is mainly due to the insufficient number of iterations of their numerical method in the experiments. In addition, HS method can still generate very accurate OF as long as sufficient iterations (i.e., several thousands) are applied. However, the gradient-based methods suffer from some problems, such as illumination variations, image motion in vicinity of motion discontinuities (i.e., due to smoothness assumption), image aliasing, and noise [108]. According to the assumptions of the first-order Taylor approximation and the intensity conservation, the OF's basic equation is as follows [109] :

$$\frac{\partial I}{\partial x}\frac{dx}{dt} + \frac{\partial I}{\partial y}\frac{dy}{dt} + \frac{\partial I}{\partial t} = 0 \qquad (2.9)$$

This Eq. (2.9) can be transformed to another form shown in Eq. (2.10) :

$$I_x u + I_y v + I_t = 0 \qquad (2.10)$$

Yang et al. [109] also declared that, $I(x, y, t)$ represents the continuous space-time intensity distributing function of a given image. I_x and I_y, are the x gradient and y gradient of image I, respectively. In addition, I_t represents partial differentiation towards the time, and (u, v) indicates the components of the image velocity field.

In order to end up with dense flow estimates one may embed the OF constraint into a regularization framework. In the Horn and Schunck's study [101], they declared that the OF problem involves minimizing a combination of the OF constraint and a smoothness term [107]. They proposed the regularization method that it involves minimizing an energy functional of the following form [108, 110] :

$$E(u, v) = \int_{\Omega} \left(I_x u + I_y v + I_t\right)^2 + \lambda \left(u_x^2 + u_y^2 + v_x^2 + v_y^2\right) dx \qquad (2.11)$$

In Eq. (2.11), I is the image intensity function, $[u(x, t), v(x, t)]^T$ is the motion vector to be estimated, subscripts x, y, and t denote the direction in the partial derivatives, $x = [x, y]^T$ is a point in the spatial domain, Ω represents the 2D image domain and λ is a parameter controlling the degree of smoothness in the flow field [108]. Also, smoothness weight $\lambda > 0$ serves as regularization parameter: Larger values for λ result in a stronger penalization of large flow gradients and lead to smoother flow fields [110]. In dense flow fields, this regularization is a clear advantage over local methods. In addition, the gradient-based methods are sensitive to the image noise inherited from gradient measurement. The reader may refer for more detailed information about HS method to the studies of Teng et al. [108] and Bruhn et al. [110], respectively.

2.4.2 Lucas–Kanade Technique (Sparse OF)

There is a problem with the subdimensionality of the OF formulation in Eq. (2.11). Therefore, Lucas and Kanade [102] proposed another method to solve the problem on small local windows where the motion vector is assumed to be constant [111]. The LK method involves minimizing the equation of the following form:

$$\sum Z^2(x) \left[E_x u + E_y v + E_t\right]^2. \qquad (2.12)$$

In Eq. (2.12), E is the pixel intensity, Z is a weighted window, and u and v are the motion vectors toward x and y directions [111]. When we look at details so that the goal of LK method is to align a template image $T(\mathbf{x})$ to an input image $I(\mathbf{x})$. Also, $\mathbf{x} = (x, y)^T$ is a column vector containing the pixel coordinates. According to the study of Baker and Matthews [112], if the LK algorithm is being used to compute OF or to track an image patch from time $t = 1$ to time $t = 2$ the template $T(\mathbf{x})$ is an extracted subregion (e.g., a 5×5 window) of the image at $t = 1$ and $I(\mathbf{x})$ is the image at $t = 2$. Baker and Matthews discussed about the parameterized set of allowed warps, which is denoted as $\mathbf{W}(\mathbf{x}; \mathbf{p})$. Also, $\mathbf{p} = (p_1, \ldots, p_n)^T$ is a parameter vector. The warp $\mathbf{W}(\mathbf{x}; \mathbf{p})$ takes the pixel $\mathbf{x}$ in the coordinates frame of the template T. Therefore, the warp maps it to the subpixel location $\mathbf{W}(\mathbf{x}; \mathbf{p})$ in the coordinate frame of the image I. As we mentioned before, the LK algorithm aims to minimize the sum of squared error between two images, the template T and the image I warped back onto the coordinate frame of the template [112]. The mathematical expression is given as Eq. (2.13):

$$\sum_{x} = \left[I\left(\mathbf{W}(\mathbf{x}; \mathbf{p})\right) - T\left(\mathbf{x}\right) \right]^{2}. \qquad (2.13)$$

In addition, warping I back to compute $I\left(\mathbf{W}(\mathbf{x}; \mathbf{p})\right)$ requires interpolating the image I at the subpixel locations $\mathbf{W}(\mathbf{x}; \mathbf{p})$. The minimization of the expression in Eq. (2.13) is performed with respect to $\mathbf{p}$ and the sum is performed over all of the pixels $\mathbf{x}$ in the template image $T\left(\mathbf{x}\right)$. The reader may refer for more detailed information about LK method to the studies of Sahba et al. [111], and Baker and Matthews [112].

According to the study of Yin et al. [113], in order to reduce computational cost, image corner detection is frequently used in OF-based trackers. Also, the pyramid implementation is often used in the literature (e.g., the OpenCV's implementation is simply based on Gaussian pyramidal decomposition of the image, which calculates coordinates of the feature points on the current video frame given their coordinates on the previous frame. The OpenCV's function finds the coordinates with subpixel accuracy [77]). When one looks at the details for corner detection, the extraction of the feature points is the key to effectively track the moving object(s). Therefore, the corner detection can be used to track target object(s). In the literature, the frequently used corner detection schemes are KLT detection [104, 113] and Harris corner detection [22, 113]. The Harris scheme is usually sensitive to the noise. In general, suppose image A is a given image for KLT computation, the second order moment matrix G can be constructed by KLT algorithm as following:

$$G = \sum_{x=u_x-\omega_x}^{u_x+\omega_x} \sum_{y=u_y-\omega_y}^{u_y+\omega_y} \begin{bmatrix} I_x^2 & I_x I_y \\ I_x I_y & I_y^2 \end{bmatrix} \qquad (2.14)$$

In Eq. (2.14), ω_x and ω_y is the parameter of window size. The size of the window is $[(2\omega_x + 1)\ (2\omega_y + 1)]$, and (x, y) is the pixel location. Also, I_x and I_y can be computed as given below:

$$I_x = \frac{A(x+1,y)-A(x-1,y)}{2}$$
$$\qquad (2.15)$$
$$I_y = \frac{A(x,y+1)-A(x,y-1)}{2}$$

The reader may refer to the studies of Bradski and Kaehler [77] and Yin et al. [113] for more details of the corner detection (i.e., KLT tracker) and LK OF algorithm based on the pyramidal implementation.

2.4.3 Literature Review

In the literature, the OF method is frequently used in image motion analysis. The computation of OF from an image sequence provides very important information for motion analysis. This issue involves moving object D&T, moving object segmentation, and motion recognition [107]. In the study of Lai [107], a new motion estimation algorithm was presented that it provides accurate OF computation under nonuniform brightness variations. The proposed algorithm is based on a regularization formulation that minimizes a combination of a modified data constraint energy and a smoothness measure all over the image domain. In the study, the data constraint was derived from the conservation of the Laplacian of Gaussian (LoG) filtered image function, which alleviates the problem with the traditional brightness constancy assumption under nonuniform illumination variations. Also, the resulting energy minimization was accomplished by an incomplete Cholesky preconditioned conjugate gradient algorithm. According to Lai, the comparisons of experimental results on benchmarking image sequences by using the proposed algorithm and some of the best existing methods were given to its superior performance [107].

Teng et al. [108] presented a very accurate algorithm for computing OF with nonuniform brightness variations that the proposed algorithm is based on a generalized dynamic image model in conjunction with a regularization framework to cope with the problem of nonuniform brightness variations. Also, they employed a reweighted least-squares method to suppress unreliable flow constraints to alleviate flow constraint errors due to image aliasing and noise, thus leading to robust estimation of OF. In addition, they proposed a dynamic smoothness adjustment scheme, and also employed a constraint refinement scheme to reduce the approximation errors in the first-order differential flow equation. According to Teng et al. [108], the experimental results show that their proposed algorithm compares most favorably to the existing techniques reported in the literature in terms of accuracy in OF computation with 100 % density.

Myocardial motion is directly related to cardiac (i.e., heart) vascular supply. Also, it can be helpful in diagnosing the heart abnormalities. In addition, the most comprehensive and available imaging study of the cardiac function is B-Mode echocardiography [111]. According to the study of Sahba et al. [111], most of the previous motion estimation methods suffer from shear, rotation, and wide range of motions due to the complexity of the myocardial motion in B-Mode images. They introduced a hybrid method based on a new algorithm that it called combined local global OF which is in combination with multiresolution spatiotemporal spline moments. Also, it is used in order to increase the accuracy and robustness to shear, rotation, and wide range of motions. In their study, the experimental results demonstrated a better efficiency with respect to other B-Mode echocardiography motion estimation techniques such as LK, HS and spatiotemporal affine technique.

In the study of Yin et al. [113], in order to realize the detection of the mobile object with camouflage color, a scheme based on OF model was put forward. At first, the OF model was used to model the motion pattern of the object and the background. Then, the magnitude and the location of the OF were used to cluster the motion pattern, and the object detection result was obtained. At the end, the location and scale of the object were used as the state variables. Also, the Kalman filter was used to improve the performance of the detection, and the final detection result was obtained. According to the study of Yin et al. [113], the experimental results show that the algorithm can solve the mobile object detection satisfactorily.

According to the study of Madjidi and Negahdaripour [114], despite high variability in the conditions of various bodies of water, a simplified image model allows the researchers to draw general conclusions on the computation of visual motion from color channels, based on average common medium characteristics. The model offers insight into information encoded in various color channels, advantages in the use of a certain color representation over others, consistency between conclusions from the theoretical study, and from experiments with data sets recoded in various types of ocean waters and locations. Their study concludes that OF computation based on the *HSV* representation typically provides more improved localization and motion estimation precision relative to other color presentations. In their study, results of various experiments with underwater data were given to assess the accuracy [114].

Amiaz et al. [115] presented a readily applicable way to go beyond the accuracy limits of current OF estimators. According to Amiaz et al., modern OF algorithms employ the coarse to fine approach. Also, they suggested to upgrade this class of algorithms, by adding over-fine interpolated levels to the pyramid. In addition, theoretical analysis of the coarse to over-fine approach explains its advantages in handling flow-field discontinuities and simulations show its benefit for subpixel motion. They reduced the estimation error by 10–30 % on the common test sequences by applying the suggested technique to various multiscale OF algorithms. Using the coarse to over-fine technique, they obtained OF estimation results that are currently the best for benchmark sequences.

Kalmoun et al. [116] considered in their study the problem of 3D OF computation in real time. The 3D OF model was derived from a straightforward extension of the 2D HS model and discretized using standard finite differences. They compared the memory costs and convergence rates of four numerical schemes: Gauss–Seidel and multigrid with three different strategies of coarse grid operators discretization: direct coarsening, lumping, and Galerkin approaches. According to the study of Kalmoun et al. [116], the experimental results to compute 3D motion from cardiac C-arm computed tomography (CT) images demonstrated that their variational multigrid based on Galerkin discretization outperformed significantly the Gauss–Seidel method. In addition, the parallel implementation of the proposed scheme using domain partitioning shows that the algorithm scales well up to 32 processors on a cluster [116].

Fernández-Caballero et al. [117] introduced a new approach to real-time human detection. The approach process the video captured by a thermal infrared camera mounted on the autonomous mobile platform. Their approach starts with a phase of static analysis for the detection of human candidates through some classical image processing techniques. These techniques are the image normalization and thresholding, etc. Then, their proposal starts a dynamic image analysis phase based in OF or image difference. In their study, LK OF was used when the robot is moving, while image difference is the preferred method when the mobile platform is still. The results of both phases were compared to enhance the human segmentation by infrared camera.

Chapter 3
A Software Approach to Performance Evaluation

Abstract This chapter provides four sections. The first section introduces the ViCamPEv software infrastructure (i.e., OpenCV, etc.), the CAVIAR video dataset, and its CVML (i.e., XML GT file format), and some other studies in the literature (e.g., MERL-PEP platform). In the second section, the architectural overview of the ViCamPEv software is presented and how the GT data is used to measure and evaluate the performance of given object D&T methods. Also, UML-based component diagram of software and the development platform of software are presented. In the third section, the testing conditions and testbed (i.e., software and hardware) are explained, and detailed via the screenshots of ViCamPEv's GUI windows. In the fourth section, the system workflow is given via two parts of ViCamPEv: the Camera part and the Video part. The system is treated as automatic or semi-automatic test environment, which combines the input data with parameters of given methods.

Keywords Test environment · ViCamPEv · Graphical user interface · CAVIAR · OpenCV

3.1 Introduction

The ViCamPEv software is available at http://efe.ege.edu.tr/~karasulu/vicampev/ and http://members.comu.edu.tr/bkarasulu/EgeWeb/wwwhome/vicampev/ with the necessary files [118]. The ViCamPEv software has the ability to measure the performance of algorithms of three popular object detection and tracking (D&T) methods. It supports the analysis of these algorithms for different parameters. Therefore, it displays their results. The best performance comparison of people D&T methods in an invariant medium is the underlying theory of our evaluation platform (i.e., proposed software). In addition, the invariant medium should be selected as non-affective from changes in noise and lighting condition [17].

B. Karasulu and S. Korukoglu, *Performance Evaluation Software*, SpringerBriefs
in Computer Science, DOI: 10.1007/978-1-4614-6534-8_3, © The Author(s) 2013

When we need the best results for our tests, we expect our test medium to be ideal. Furthermore, the comparisons of object D&T algorithms can be easily made via an ideal medium. The CAVIAR database is so far an ideal medium with little faults [17]. For the video part of our software, we have used first the dataset of CAVIAR database for performance testing. The camera part of our software does not provide or use such ideal medium because of its real-time conditions. The ViCamPEv software works with CAVIAR's GT XML file format. This database's datasets are suitable only for people D&T. Our software is based on OpenCV infrastructure. In version 0.03, it already takes uncompressed AVI and/or compressed MPEG file format for input via OpenCV v2.4.1 infrastructure [17]. Our software works as automatic and/or semi-automatic test environment (ATE and/or SATE). The ViCamPEv can compare the performance results of two methods in the same plot if one of the results of the method's performance was saved by the end-user prior to the testing process [17].

In the literature, there are situation-specific methods. Generally, the BS method is used frequently for videos of visual surveillance systems and the CMS method is used for D&T of the human face. Both the methods have advantages and disadvantages. These methods' performance is measured by using different metrics. These metrics are based on the blob or point set and/or based on the bounding box area. In addition, there is a great variety in metrics to analyze and contrast the various algorithms and approaches. We have designed our software to make a remarkable consensus on differences in object D&T methods, which is made via same performance metrics at the same platform [17].

Researchers have used some common and specific metrics in the literature. In the Bashir and Porikli [45] study based on MERL-PEP [41] platform, they have defined some frame-based and object-based metrics. The reader may refer to their study [45] and their website [41] as well. They have used PETS [53] and in-house (i.e., their own data) datasets [17]. When researchers want to compare our ViCamPEv platform with MERL-PEP platform based on the metrics, they can see that the metrics are not identical because of their point of view [17, 118]. The definitions and details of our metrics are given in Chap. 4. In addition, Bashir and Porikli made only their experiments for Ensemble and Multi-kernel MS tracking system. Therefore, researchers are unable to compare the other methods (i.e., BS, pure CMS, Dense OF, and Sparse OF) with their results.

Sacan et al. [18] expressed that the CellTrack software allows exportation of the tracking results of cell motility as raw text data or as movie or image files. The analysis of tracking via CellTrack does not involve a performance measurement and/or evaluation. Our software aims to measure and evaluate the performance of the above-mentioned object D&T methods.

Our study is different from that of Bashir and Porikli [45] (and MERL-PEP platform [41]) and from that of Sacan et al. [18]. The distinguishing features of our study are ViCamPEv software ATE and/or SATE capability, interactive and automatic D&T support, real-time performance measurement capabilities, support for three popular methods at the same platform, and support for the set of the same metrics for these three popular methods, respectively. For more details, the reader may refer to Karasulu and Korukoglu [17].

3.2 Architecture Overview

The ViCamPEv software consists of five main modules. These modules are video playing, performance measuring, XML file loading/viewing, results charting/plotting, and reporting module [17]. The OpenCV [77, 78] has a library called HighGUI. It is a kind of Graphical User Interface (GUI). There are some specific utilities provided by OpenCV via HighGUI, which are reading video from disk, capturing video from cameras, or loading still images from files. The video playing module is responsible for accurately playing of video resource. This video resource is a camera stream (i.e., sequence) or a videoclip file. The module controls video playing, stopping, recording, and restarting the played video, and it is also responsible for starting of each of the object D&T methods on tracking menu by selection of end-user. Thence, object D&T processes start and end via this module. The video playing module works with BS, CMS, Dense OF and Sparse OF methods. The performance measuring module takes responsibility for measuring object D&T algorithm performances and their evaluation, which consists of 16 performance metric-based methods. The performance measuring module provides the ability of saving the performance results and loading the previously saved performance results in run-time [17].

The XML file loading/viewing module is responsible for loading appropriate XML files of CAVIAR onto system, it also shows these GT data in an appropriate and human-understandable format to end-user. The performance measuring module takes GT data information as an input. This module gives the derived results to the performance results charting/plotting module. When the results charting/plotting module takes all of the results from performance measuring module, it shows evaluation results to end-user via plots. The overall and other results of video sequence are presented by performance reporting module in a report format. When end-user wants to save or print performance results and/or report, the relevant module also provides related options for outputs [17].

In our software, the video instance is played in video-time, but the camera instance is played in real-time. For the video part, the performance measurement is made only for video instance via predefined GT data. For the camera part, there is no performance measurement because of the absence of GT data. The performance measurements are obtained in real-time by our software via video playing. It can be shown graphically while the relevant videoclip is still playing. The results of performance measurements are recorded in video-time because of the video frame-based comparison. For more details about real-time and video-time terms, the reader may refer to Karasulu and Korukoglu [17]. The comparison is made for object D&T performance result among different algorithms. Figure 3.1 shows an overview of our software system [17]. It is described in component diagram form of the Unified Modeling Language (UML) v2.2.

The ViCamPEv application is user friendly and supports interactive and automatic object D&T methods. Tracking menu controls the progression of the algorithm. Also, the parameters panel (i.e., right panel) controls parameter settings as a part of GUI. Relevant controls and trackbars for BS, CMS, Dense OF, and Sparse OF method

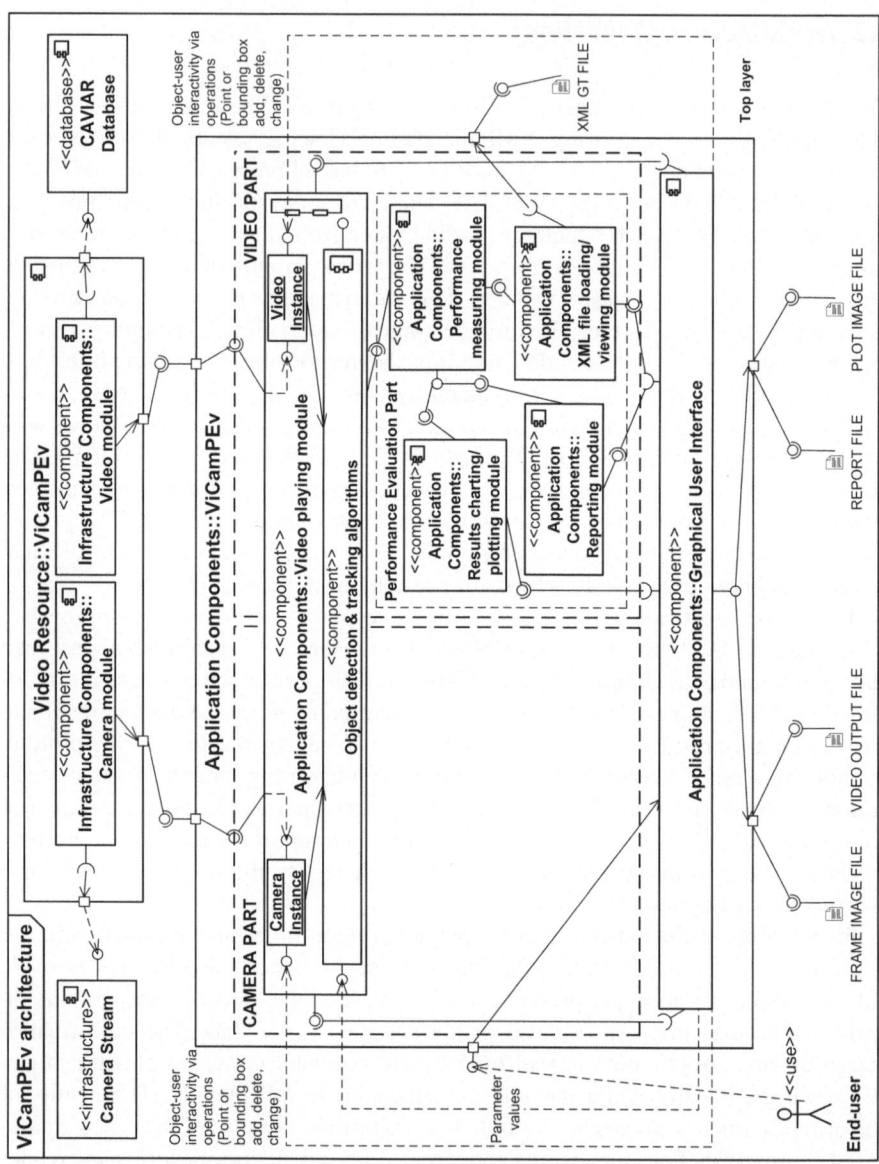

Fig. 3.1 Architectural design (i.e., component diagram) of our ViCamPEv software [17]

are available via parameters panel for end-user's usage [17]. In our study, there are three different BS variants. They are videomode1, videomode2, and videomode3. Thence, BS's videomode1 is based on *pure* background averaging method. Also, BS's videomode2 is a combination. It is based on frame-by-frame running average difference computation (RADC) of videomode1. BS's videomode3 is based only on

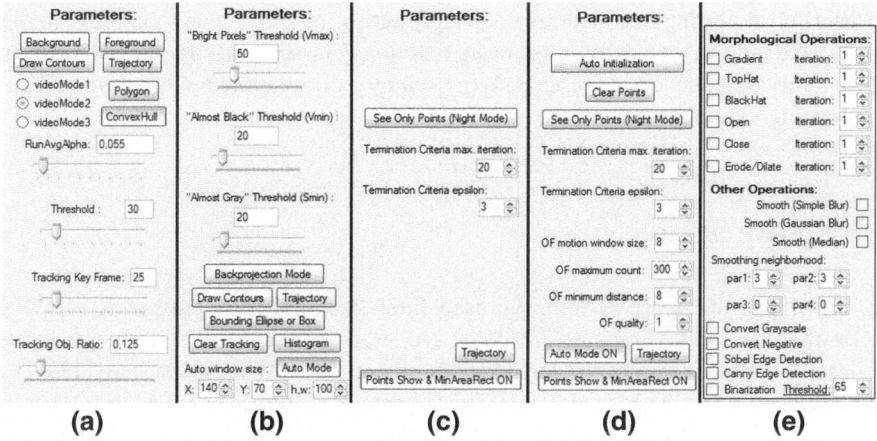

Fig. 3.2 The parts of ViCamPEv's GUI [17], **a** shows the parameters panel for BS method, **b** shows the panel for CMS method, **c** shows the panel for Dense OF method, **d** shows the panel for Sparse OF method, **e** shows the morphology panel

pure frame-by-frame RADC method. Therefore, these three different methods show different D&T and performance results as BS variants [17]. Testing processes are constructed using the main screen of ViCamPEv. This screen involves controls on the bottom and right panels. Mouse events are used to add/delete or change operations on objects and change pixel-based locations and/or object IDs of them in D&T process or performance measurement. The bottom panel controls the video playing, recording, etc.

In Chap. 5, BS method's performance testing results of our study are given in tables only for BS's videomode1. The GUI panel(s) settings for all object D&T methods are shown as each method's parameter settings while each method is running. All the algorithms of object D&T methods in our software are able to work with or without GT data. The morphological operations of GUI (at the morphology panel) help the end-user to apply some filters and effects on videoclip's current playing frame in real-time. For more details, the reader may refer to Karasulu and Korukoglu [17]. In our study, we focus on videoclips and their GT data for performance evaluation, but we have added camera functions for object D&T algorithms provided by ViCamPEv system. They are used for all purposes except as performance evaluation by end-user in experimental camera mode. Figure 3.2 shows GUI's main screen's parts [17], which are Fig. 3.2a parameters (i.e., right) panel for BS method, Fig. 3.2b for CMS method, Fig. 3.2c for Dense OF method, Fig. 3.2d for Sparse OF method, Fig. 3.2e the morphology panel.

In our study, we have designed our software based on both an *object-oriented* and a *modular* infrastructure. Object-oriented Visual C++ language is used in the process of software development. Object orientation makes the software more flexible and reusable. In this scope, maintaining and modification of existing source code is easy. In our study, the ViCamPEv software modules are designed in a complementary manner, which are designed to complete each other in our software. The performance measuring, reporting, and results charting/plotting modules share *common items*, such as data types, type definitions, basic functions/classes, and structures. However, these items are defined (i.e., produced) or used by video playing module and/or XML file loading/viewing module.

3.3 System Setup

In our testing hardware system, we used Intel Pentium IV processor at 3.0 GHz, 3 Gb of RAM, and Microsoft Windows 7 operating system. The software source codes are compiled with Microsoft Visual Studio 2010 on Windows system [17]. The image processing and video playing infrastructure of system is based on the OpenCV library [77, 78]. The performance result plots are based on freeware charting/plotting scientific Nplot library [119]. In addition, plots can be saved as a separate image file by end-user or printed out via our system. Testing processes are applied on CAVIAR database's first scenario, which is called INRIA entrance hall [46]. In Fig. 3.3, a snapshot of GUI main screen of our software is shown during the playback of *Browse2* videoclip in normal video show mode with GT data [17].

Figure 3.4 shows some GUI windows of ViCamPEv application. In Fig. 3.4a, the XML viewer window is shown while viewing of *Fight_Chase* videoclip's GT XML file. In Fig. 3.4b, the performance result's plot window is shown for a testing process (via BS method), which used *Fight_Chase* videoclip and its GT data [17]. These figures are based on the working processes of ViCamPEv software [118].

Fig. 3.3 A snapshot of ViCamPEv software's GUI main screen [17]

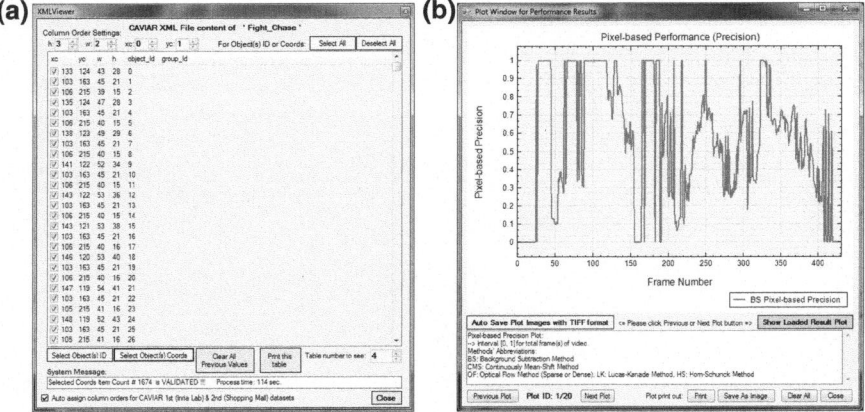

Fig. 3.4 The GUI windows of ViCamPEv, **a** shows the XMLViewer window snapshot while viewing and loading GT data on to system, **b** shows the performance result's plot window's snapshot during a testing process [17]

3.4 System Workflow

In our study, the system has two main entry points (i.e., input resource). Also, our system uses some kind of data. They are used as input data of ATE or SATE. The temporal information of given video frame and pixel values of the frame are these data. These entry points are based on resource type, such as camera stream or videoclip. Also, the ATE/SATE combines these data with the relevant object D&T algorithm and its parameters. They are chosen and adjusted by the software or by end-user [17]. Furthermore, ViCamPEv application has two main parts: Camera part and Video part. While playing a camera stream or a videoclip, processing object D&T method can be instantaneously changed by end-user via GUI. However, end-user should not wait for an object D&T method's working to be finished. When end-user desires to change the currently working method, he/she can just change the method via relevant menu item on the tracking menu. Our system converts GT data from XML tables and columns to appropriate data format for performance measurement of the chosen object D&T method's algorithm. In addition, the plots of performance results, report file, and/or an output of tracked camera stream or videoclip are outputs of ViCamPEv system [17].

Chapter 4
Performance Measures and Evaluation

Abstract This chapter provides two sections. The first section introduces our performance evaluation methodology. The second section is separated into three subsections, which are frame-based detection measures, measures based on object matching criteria, and object tracking-based measures, respectively. In our study, some performance measures are used to evaluate object D&T method's performance. In this manner, the measures for frame-based detection are object count accuracy, pixel-based precision, pixel-based recall, pixel-based F1 measure, area-based precision, area-based recall, area-thresholded precision, area-thresholded recall, and average fragmentation, respectively. Also, the measures based on object matching criteria are sequence frame detection accuracy, and position-based, size-based, and orientation-based measures, respectively. In addition, the measures based on object tracking are the object count-based measure, temporal measure, and sequence tracking detection accuracy, respectively. All of the above-mentioned measures are given via mathematical background in related subsections of this book.

Keywords Frame-based detection · Object matching criteria · Object tracking · Performance · Evaluation

4.1 Introduction

For video surveillance systems, related performance evaluation projects provide a benchmark set of annotated video sequences. Some different indoor and outdoor scenarios are involved by these benchmark datasets. Object detection and tracking (D&T) algorithms have to be evaluated for related scenario type. In these performance evaluations, there are some metrics [17]. Thirde et al. discussed about a kind of evaluation methodology. It is based on the object-level evaluation [120, 121]. Principally, our evaluation methodology is mostly based on VACE metrics [54]. It can be considered both as an object-based evaluation and as a frame-based evaluation. According

B. Karasulu and S. Korukoglu, *Performance Evaluation Software*, SpringerBriefs in Computer Science, DOI: 10.1007/978-1-4614-6534-8_4, © The Author(s) 2013

to Lazarevic–McManus et al. [40] and Baumann et al. [43], an object-based performance analysis does not provide essential true negative objects. Therefore, receiver operating characteristic (ROC) optimization cannot be used. They suggest using F-measure when ROC optimization is not appropriate [17]. Also, VACE Phase II metrics are declared in supplementary evaluation protocol document of the study of Kasturi et al. [39].

4.2 Evaluation Metrics Used in the Proposed Approach

In order to analyze quantitatively the performance of our people (i.e., object) D&T software, we have implemented a set of performance metrics. In ViCamPEv software [17], we considered several metrics found in the literature [39, 43]. In our evaluation platform, frame-based metrics are object count accuracy (OCA), pixel-based and area-based precision and recall (PBP, ABP, PBR and ABR, respectively), area-thresholded precision and recall (ATP, ATR), average fragmentation (AF), pixel-based F1 measure (PBF1).

Let DTO be the detected object (result of an algorithm) and GTO be the ground-truth object. In our evaluation platform, some measures are for matched sets of DTOs and GTOs. They are position-based (PBM), size-based (SBM), orientation-based (OBM) measures, and sequence frame detection accuracy (SFDA), which are frame-based metrics. Also, their matching criteria are given in Sect. 4.2.2. Object-based metrics are object count-based F2 measure (OCBF2), temporal F3 measure (TempF3), spatio-temporal matching (i.e., Sequence Tracking Detection Accuracy (STDA)). Above-mentioned metrics are normalized in a range between *one* and *zero*. Therefore, they have a value for every frame of relevant video sequence within a range from *zero* to *one*. The *zero* value indicates the *worst* performance result and *one* value indicates the *best* performance result for relevant object D&T algorithm. For many metrics, when a metric's value close to *one*, the developers or testers of D&T methods can determine how good is the accuracy and/or robustness of relevant D&T method [17].

The general precision (P) and recall (R) concept are given in Eqs. (4.1) and (4.2), where false negative, false positive, and true positive are abbreviated as FN, FP and TP, respectively. Where the | | operator represents the number of pixels or detections in the relevant image area. For more detail of P and R measures, the reader may refer to Lazarevic–McManus et al. study [17, 40]

$$Precision = \frac{|TP|}{|TP| + |FP|} \tag{4.1}$$

$$Recall = \frac{|TP|}{|TP| + |FN|} \tag{4.2}$$

In our evaluation platform, a set of some metrics are developed. This set is in a form of mixture of general VACE Phase II metrics and some other metrics in the literature. These metrics are PBF1, OCBF2 and TempF3, and given in more detail in Sects. 4.2.1 and 4.2.3, respectively. In Sect. 4.2.2, object matching criteria are given in more detail. In our study, these criteria are used for both frame-based and object-based metrics. For all of the above-mentioned metrics, their methodology of evaluation and object matching criteria are explained in more detail in this chapter. In addition, the reader may refer to the study of Kasturi et al. [39] for more details of use of general metrics based on VACE Phase II and other metrics [17].

4.2.1 Frame-Based Detection Measures

Some frame-based detection metrics are used in our study as given below. Some of them are based on VACE Phase II metrics. Generally, in these metrics, the *Null* term represents the empty set, and the | | operator represents the number of pixels in relevant area [17]. In addition, these metrics are used to develop a new metric by us. This new metric is called PBF1.

Object Count Accuracy: Let GTO(t) be the set of GT objects in a single frame t and let DTO(t) be the set of output boxes, which are results of an algorithm in that frame. The object count accuracy (OCA) for frame t is defined as [17]:

$$OCA(t) = \begin{cases} \text{undefined} & , \quad if \quad N_{GTO}(t) + N_{DTO}(t) = 0 \\ \frac{Minimum(N_{GTO}(t),N_{DTO}(t))}{\frac{N_{GTO}(t)+N_{DTO}(t)}{2}} & , \quad otherwise \end{cases} \tag{4.3}$$

where N_{DTO} and N_{GTO} are the numbers of output boxes and ground-truth objects in frame t, respectively. Only the count of boxes in each frame is considered in this measure, but spatial information is not considered. Overall OCA is defined as the average OCA(t) over all frames [39].

Pixel-based Precision: Let the ratio of detected areas in GT with total detection be Pixel-based Precision (PBP). The PBP for frame t is defined as [17]:

$$PBP(t) = \begin{cases} \text{undefined} & , \quad if \quad Union_{DTO}(t) = Null \\ 1 - \frac{|Union_{DTO}(t) \cap \overline{Union_{GTO}(t)}|}{Union_{DTO}(t)} & , \quad otherwise \end{cases} \tag{4.4}$$

where $Union_{DTO}(t)$ and $Union_{GTO}(t)$ are the spatial union of boxes in DTO(t) and GTO(t), respectively. $DTO_i(t)$ and $GTO_i(t)$ represent ith DTO and GTO in the tth frame, respectively [17, 39].

$$Union_{GTO}(t) = \bigcup_{i=1}^{N_{GTO}(t)} GTO_i(t) \tag{4.5}$$

$$Union_{DTO}(t) = \bigcup_{i=1}^{N_{DTO}(t)} DTO_i(t) \tag{4.6}$$

If the researchers need the weighted average precision of all the frames in sequence, they must compute the overall PBP.

$OverallPBP(t)$

$$= \begin{cases} undefined & , \quad if \quad \sum_{t=1}^{N_{frames}} |Union_{DTO}(t)| = 0 \\ \frac{\sum_{t=1}^{N_{frames}} |Union_{DTO}(t)| \times PBP(t)}{\sum_{t=1}^{N_{frames}} |Union_{DTO}(t)|} & , \quad otherwise \end{cases} \tag{4.7}$$

where N_{frames} is the number of frames in the GT data set [17, 39].

Pixel-based Recall: The Pixel-based Recall (PBR) measure measures how well the algorithm minimizes FNs. PBR is defined as [17, 39]:

$$PBR(t) = \begin{cases} undefined & , \quad if \quad Union_{GTO}(t) = Null \\ 1 - \frac{|Union_{GTO}(t) \cap \overline{Union_{DTO}(t)}|}{Union_{GTO}(t)} & , \quad otherwise \end{cases} \tag{4.8}$$

If the researchers need the weighted average recall of all the frames in sequence, they must compute the overall PBR.

$OverallPBR(t)$

$$= \begin{cases} undefined & , \quad if \quad \sum_{t=1}^{N_{frames}} |Union_{GTO}(t)| = 0 \\ \frac{\sum_{t=1}^{N_{frames}} |Union_{GTO}(t)| \times PBR(t)}{\sum_{t=1}^{N_{frames}} |Union_{GTO}(t)|} & , \quad otherwise \end{cases} \tag{4.9}$$

where N_{frames} is the number of frames in the GT data set [17, 39].

Pixel-based F1 Measure: According to precision/recall statistics (PR-statistics), precision and recall measure values are normally evaluated separately. When different D&T algorithms are compared at one platform with P and R measures, F-Measure (or effectiveness measure) for performance measurement is frequently desirable [122]. Our pixel-based $F1$ comparison measure is defined as [17]:

$$F1 = \frac{(1+\alpha)PR}{\alpha(P+R)} \tag{4.10}$$

where α is a parameter for relative importance (i.e., balance) of P and R values. By setting $\alpha = 1$ one obtains the commonly used balanced F-measure, i.e., the harmonic mean of P and R values. According to Lazarevic–McManus et al. study [40], the goal of this kind comparison is to determine the optimal parameters by locating the maximum F-Measure for a given α parameter. In our study, α parameter is set to *one*. Our $F1$ comparison measure is computed with above-mentioned PBP and PBR values [17]. This metric is abbreviated as PBF1 in our book.

Area-based Precision: Let the average precision of the algorithm's output boxes DTO(t) be Area-based Precision (ABP). The ABP for frame t is defined as [17]:

$$ABP(t) = \frac{\sum_{\forall DTO_i(t)} BoxPrecision(DTO_i(t))}{N_{DTO(t)}} \tag{4.11}$$

where

$$BoxPrecision(DTO_i(t)) = \frac{|DTO_i(t) \cap Union_{GTO}(t)|}{|DTO_i(t)|} \tag{4.12}$$

Overall ABP is the weighted average precision of all of the frames [17, 39].

$$OverallABP = \frac{\sum_{t=1}^{N_{frames}} N_{DTO(t)} \times ABP(t)}{\sum_{t=1}^{N_{frames}} N_{DTO(t)}} \tag{4.13}$$

Area-based Recall: Let the average recall for all the objects the GTO(t) be Area-based Recall (ABR). The ABR for frame t is defined as [17]:

$$ABR(t) = \frac{\sum_{\forall GTO_i(t)} ObjectRecall(GTO_i(t))}{N_{GTO(t)}} \tag{4.14}$$

where

$$ObjectRecall(GTO_i(t)) = \frac{|GTO_i(t) \cap Union_{DTO}(t)|}{|GTO_i(t)|} \tag{4.15}$$

Overall ABR is the weighted average recall of all of the frames [17, 39].

$$OverallABR = \frac{\sum_{t=1}^{N_{frames}} N_{GTO(t)} \times ABR(t)}{\sum_{t=1}^{N_{frames}} N_{GTO(t)}} \tag{4.16}$$

Area-thresholded Precision: The Area-thresholded Precision (ATP) is the number of output boxes that significantly covered the GTO in frame t. When a minimum proportion of area of $DTO_i(t)$ output box overlaps with $Union_{GTO}(t)$, the ATP is defined as [17]:

$$ATP(t) = \sum_{\forall GTO_i(t)} BoxPrecision(DTO_i(t)) \tag{4.17}$$

where

$$BoxPrecision(DTO_i(t)) = \begin{cases} 1 \, , & if \ \frac{|DTO_i(t) \cap Union_{GTO}(t)|}{|DTO_i(t)|} > Overlap\_min \\ 0 \, , & otherwise \end{cases} \quad (4.18)$$

Here, *Overlap_min* is the minimum proportion of the DTO's area. This area should be overlapped by the GTO, and thus the output box is precise. Overall ATP is the ratio of precise output boxes with the total number of output boxes produced by the algorithm [17, 39].

Area-thresholded Recall: The Area-thresholded Recall (ATR) is the number of detected objects in frame *t*. The ATR is defined as [17]:

$$ATR(t) = \sum_{\forall GTO_i(t)} ObjectDetect(GTO_i(t)) \quad (4.19)$$

where

$$ObjectDetect(GTO_i(t)) = \begin{cases} 1 \, , & if \ \frac{|GTO_i(t) \cap Union_{DTO}(t)|}{|GTO_i(t)|} > Overlap\_min \\ 0 \, , & otherwise \end{cases} \quad (4.20)$$

Here, *Overlap_min* is the minimum proportion of the GTO's area. This area should be overlapped by the output boxes, and thus it is correctly detected by the algorithm. Overall ATR is the ratio of detected objects with the total number of objects in the ground-truth [17, 39].

Average Fragmentation: The fragmentation of the output boxes overlapping a GTO(*t*) in frame *t* is defined as [17]:

$$Frag(GTO_i(t)) = \begin{cases} undefined & , \quad if \ N_{DTO(t) \cap GTO_i(t)} = 0 \\ \frac{1}{1 + log_{10}(N_{DTO(t) \cap GTO_i(t)})} \, , & otherwise \end{cases} \quad (4.21)$$

Overall fragmentation is defined as average fragmentation for all GTOs in the entire video sequence [17, 39]. The average fragmentation metric is abbreviated as AF in this book.

4.2.2 Measures Based on Object Matching Criteria

In this section, we review the measures that they can be performed only when object matching approach is based on centroids. Also, this approach defines the distances that are given by the definition of the centroid-based matching criteria [17].

There are some criteria to perform matching between DTOs and GTOs via centroid's position. This approach has low computational cost. In addition, it is relatively simple [43]. According to Baumann et al. [43], $\overrightarrow{b}_{GTO}$ represents the bounding box of a GTO with centroid $\overrightarrow{x}_{GTO}$ and d_{GTO} represents the length of the bounding box's diagonal of the GTO. Also, $\overrightarrow{b}_{DTO}$ and $\overrightarrow{x}_{DTO}$ represent the bounding box and the centroid of a DTO, respectively. In our software, we have used some centroid-based matching criteria declared in Baumann et al. study as well. These criteria are given below [17]:

Criterion 1: This criterion is based on the threshold Euclidean distance between the object's centroids.

$$D_1 = |\overrightarrow{x}_{GTO} - \overrightarrow{x}_{DTO}| \tag{4.22}$$

Criterion 2: This criterion is based on minimal distances.

$$D_2 = \begin{cases} 0 & : & \overrightarrow{x}_{GTO} \text{ is inside } \overrightarrow{b}_{DTO} \\ & or \cdot & \overrightarrow{x}_{DTO} \text{ is inside } \overrightarrow{b}_{GTO} \\ min(d_{GTO,DTO}, d_{DTO,GTO}) & : & else. \end{cases} \tag{4.23}$$

Also, $d_{GTO,DTO}$ and $d_{DTO,GTO}$ are given as the distances from the centroid of one object to the closest point of the bounding box of the other object. In our comparisons, a mixture of these criteria and VACE Phase II metrics are used [17, 39].

Position-based Measure: This measure measures the Positional Accuracy (PA) of object D&T results by using the mean of distances between centers of DTOs and GTOs. Let $T_h(i, t)$ be defined as [17]:

$$T_h(i, t) = \left(\frac{(Width(GTO_i(t)) + Height(GTO_i(t)) + Width(DTO_i(t)) + Height(DTO_i(t)))}{2} \right) \tag{4.24}$$

If $DTO_i(t)$ and $GTO_i(t)$ overlap at least partially in frame t, then Distance(i, t) is defined as

$$\text{Distance}(i, t) = CityblockDistance(C(GTO_i(t)), C(DTO_i(t))) \tag{4.25}$$

where $C(x)$ denotes the center of x. Furthermore, the *CityblockDistance* term is also known as TaxiCab or Manhattan distance. If $DTO_i(t)$ and $GTO_i(t)$ do not overlap at all, then Distance(i, t) is defined as $T_h(i, t)$. The PA (or Position-based measure) is defined as [17]:

$$PA(GTO_i(t)) = 1 - \frac{\text{Distance}(i, t)}{T_h(i, t)} \tag{4.26}$$

In our book, this metric is abbreviated as PBM. The overall PA for the sequence is defined as average PBM for all GTOs in the entire video sequence [17, 39].

Size-based Measure: The Size-based Measure (SBM) is a coefficient for measurement of object size during D&T process. This measurement does not consider the other factors, such as accuracy of orientation and position. However, the high score of SBM reflects how good an algorithm measures an object's size even if this algorithm fails to measure correctly the orientation and position [17, 39]. Let $Size\_Diff_i$ be an average of weighted size difference between GTO box and DTO box of object i and this average changes within a range from 0 to 1.

$$Size\_Diff_i = \frac{|Size(GTO_i(t)) - Size(DTO_i(t))|}{Max(Size(GTO_i(t)), Size(DTO_i(t)))}, \qquad (4.27)$$

$$\text{such that } t \in (\exists(GTO_i(t) \wedge DTO_i(t))),$$

$GTO_i(t)$: Ground-truth box of object i in the tth frame.
$DTO_i(t)$: Detected box of object i in the tth frame.
$Size(GTO_i(t))$: Size of ground-truth box of object i in the tth frame.
$|\bullet|$: Absolute function.

$$SBM = 1 - \frac{1}{N} \sum_{i=1}^{N} Size\_Diff_i(t) \qquad (4.28)$$

where N represents number of objects [17].

Orientation-based Measure: The Orientation-based Measure (OBM) is a coefficient for measurement of object orientation during D&T process. This measurement does not consider the other factors, such as accuracy of size and position. However, the score of OBM reflects how good an algorithm measures an object's orientation [17]. The angle difference between DTO and GTO in given frame ranges from 0 to π. The difference can get values at minimum of 0 and maximum of π. This difference is *zero* when the algorithm perfectly measures object's orientation same as the GTO's orientation [17, 39]. Also, let $Angle\_Diff_i$ be an average angle between GTO box and DTO box of object i.

$$Angle\_Diff_i = \angle(GTO_i(t), DTO_i(t)) \qquad (4.29)$$

$\angle(GTO_i(t), DTO_i(t))$: Angle between $GTO_i(t)$ and $DTO_i(t)$, $0 \leq \angle(\cdot, \cdot) \leq \pi$

$$OBM = 1 - \frac{1}{N} \sum_{i=1}^{N} \frac{Angle\_Diff_i}{\pi} \qquad (4.30)$$

where N represents number of objects [17].

Sequence Frame Detection Accuracy: The Sequence Frame Detection Accuracy (SFDA) is an area-based measure. It penalizes false or missed detections and spatial fragmentation. It requires one-to-one mapping between DTOs and GTOs [39]. For our study, a mapping strategy (i.e., object matching) is developed. It is based on object matching approach's aforementioned 'Criterion 2' (i.e., Eq. (4.23)). Also, let $FDA(t)$ be the frame detection accuracy for a single frame t.

$$FDA(t) = \frac{OverlapRatio}{\frac{N_{GTO}+N_{DTO}}{2}} \tag{4.31}$$

where N_{DTO} and N_{GTO} are the number of output boxes and ground-truth objects, respectively. And

$$OverlapRatio = \sum_{i=1}^{N_{mapped}} \frac{|GTO_i(t) \cap DTO_i(t)|}{|GTO_i(t) \cup DTO_i(t)|} \tag{4.32}$$

where N_{mapped} represents the maximum number of one-to-one mapping between DTOs and GTOs. SFDA measure measures the $FDA(t)$ value over the considered video sequence (i.e., over all frames) exclusively [17].

$$SFDA = \frac{\sum_{t=1}^{t=N_{frames}} FDA(t)}{\sum_{t=1}^{t=N_{frames}} \exists(N_{GTO}(t) \ OR \ N_{DTO}(t))} \tag{4.33}$$

4.2.3 Object Tracking-Based Measures

At a glance, above-mentioned measures do not fully consider the spatio-temporal relation between DTOs and GTOs. In this section, we consider frame-by-frame measurements where $DTO_i(t)$ and $GTO_i(t)$ represent ith DTO and GTO in the tth frame, respectively [17]. Furthermore, $N_{DTO}(t)$ and $N_{GTO}(t)$ are the number of DTOs and GTOs for frame t, respectively. Along with $N_T(GTO_i)$ is the number of frames, which have GTO_i, in them. In our study, we have developed some new metrics given in this section. These metrics are called OCBF2 and TempF3.

Object Count-based Measure: This measure considers the frame-by-frame count of GTOs and detected boxes to measure the tracking performance, but do not consider the correspondence between them [39]. In the scope of this measurement, Precision(t) and Recall(t) for frame t are defined as [17]:

$$Precision(t) = \begin{cases} N_{GTO}(t)/N_{DTO}(t) \ , & if \ \ N_{GTO}(t) < N_{DTO}(t) \\ undefined & , \ \ if \ \ N_{DTO}(t) = 0 \\ 1 & , \ \ otherwise \end{cases} \tag{4.34}$$

$$Recall(t) = \begin{cases} N_{DTO}(t)/N_{GTO}(t) \ , & if \ \ N_{GTO}(t) > N_{DTO}(t) \\ undefined & , \ \ if \ \ N_{GTO}(t) = 0 \\ 1 & , \ \ otherwise \end{cases} \tag{4.35}$$

For combining above-mentioned count-based Precision (P) and Recall (R) values, we have developed a comparison measure. Our object count-based F2 comparison measure is defined as [17]:

$$F2 = \frac{(1 + \beta)PR}{\beta(P + R)} \tag{4.36}$$

where β is a parameter for relative importance (i.e., balance) of P and R values. In our study, β parameter is set to *one* (i.e., balanced F-measure). This metric is abbreviated as OCBF2 in our book. Overall Precision and overall Recall for the video sequence are defined as the average P and average R values over all frames [17].

Temporal Measure: This measure measures the tracking performance based on the number of detection counts for each GTO [39]. Precision and Recall for each GTO_i are defined as [17]:

$$Precision(GTO_i) = \frac{N_{TS}(GTO_i)}{N_T(DTO_i)} \tag{4.37}$$

$$Recall(GTO_i) = \frac{N_{TS}(GTO_i)}{N_T(GTO_i)} \tag{4.38}$$

where $N_T(DTO_i)$ is the number of frames where DTO_i is declared by the algorithm as detected object. The $N_{TS}(GTO_i)$ is the number of frames where GTO_i is present and declared by system. In our study, we have developed a comparison measure for combining temporal measure-based Precision (P) and Recall (R) values. Our temporal F3 comparison measure is defined as [17]:

$$F3 = \frac{(1 + \gamma)PR}{\gamma(P + R)} \tag{4.39}$$

where γ is a parameter for relative importance (i.e., balance) of P and R values. In our study, γ parameter is set to *one* (i.e., balanced F-measure). Also, this metric is abbreviated as TempF3 in our book. Overall Precision and overall Recall for the sequence are defined as the average P and average R values over all frames [17].

Sequence Tracking Detection Accuracy: The Sequence Tracking Detection Accuracy (STDA) is a spatio-temporal-based measure [39]. We have used one-to-one mapping strategy for this measure like our object-matching strategy that we applied to SFDA measure as well. Tracking Detection Accuracy (TDA) is defined as [17]:

$$TDA = \sum_{i=1}^{N_{frames}} \frac{|GTO_i(t) \cap DTO_i(t)|}{|GTO_i(t) \cup DTO_i(t)|} \tag{4.40}$$

where N_{frames} is the total number of ground-truth frames in the sequence. The STDA is defined as [17]:

$$STDA = \sum_{i=1}^{N_{mapped}} \frac{\sum_{i=1}^{N_{frames}} \left[\frac{|GTO_i(t) \cap DTO_i(t)|}{|GTO_i(t) \cup DTO_i(t)|} \right]}{N(GTO_i \cup DTO_i \neq Null)} \qquad (4.41)$$

where N_{mapped} represents the maximum number of one-to-one mapping between DTOs and GTOs. Furthermore, the Average Tracking Accuracy (ATA) is another metric. It can be termed as the STDA per object. The ATA(t) is defined as [17]:

$$ATA(t) = \frac{STDA}{\frac{N_{GTO}(t) + N_{DTO}(t)}{2}} \qquad (4.42)$$

Overall ATA is defined as the average ATA(t) over all frames.

Chapter 5
A Case Study: People Detection and Tracking in Videos

Abstract This chapter provides three sections. The first section introduces the video database that it is used in our experiments. This database is based on people surveillance footage and called CAVIAR. In our study, the performance results are based on both qualitative and quantitative evaluation. In second section, some experimental results of our study are presented via qualitative and overall quantitative (i.e., numerical) results of performance. In addition, we explain that the capabilities of ViCamPEv are used to obtain these results. In third section, we present both statistical and algorithmic analysis of relevant object D&T methods. These methods are comparable via the results in related tables for related methods. The discussion about given methods are presented through these experimental results and performance evaluation.

Keywords CAVIAR · ViCamPEv · Performance evaluation · Statistical analysis · Algorithmic analysis

5.1 Dataset

In our experiments, we have used the CAVIAR database [46]. It consists of three datasets, namely the corridor view and front view of shopping mall in Portugal, and entrance hall of INRIA laboratory in France. The CAVIAR database provides typical surveillance footage with ground-truth information. Also, the INRIA entrance hall dataset has six types of events, which are called '*Browsing*', '*Fighting*', '*Groups_meeting*', '*Leaving_bags*', '*Rest*', and '*Walking*', respectively. In this first dataset, there are totally 28 video sequences. In our study, we used 27 video sequences, because one of these videos is missing in their website. The CAVIAR database [17, 46] was selected for evaluation of algorithms of different object D&T methods because of its generality. However, it is suitable only for people D&T. The GT data of CAVIAR database for above mentioned sequences was found by hand-labeling the images and by declaring the hypothesis. The hypothesis are based on

the object's movement, role, context, and situation, etc. This is a factor for amount
of manual power in terms of time due to hand-labeling of every new GT data. It is
an error-prone process. In CAVIAR's website [46], the GT XML files are published.
They are based on CVML [50]. The infrastructure of ViCamPEv software uses these
GT data for people (i.e., object) D&T performance evaluation, and then, it shows
results on the related plot window. In our study, we focus on the INRIA entrance
hall dataset's events. These events have several video sequences and their related GT
XML files. The total frame numbers and GT XML data file name of each videoclips
of relevant event with their video number [17, 123] are given in Table 5.1.

In Table 5.1, we marked a GT XML file name (i.e., shown as a superscript star sym-
bol), which is for '*Fight_OneManDown*' videoclip, and it shows the first variant of GT
XML files for this videoclip (i.e., *fomdgt1.xml*). Also, we chose to use this first XML
file only for '*Fight_OneManDown*' videoclip, which is used for our performance

Table 5.1 Total frame numbers and GT XML file names of CAVIAR's first scenario's videoclips
given in the study [17, 123]

Video number	Events/Videoclip name	Total frame	GT XML file name
V1	Browsing / Browse1	1044	*br1gt.xml*
V2	Browsing / Browse2	876	*br2gt.xml*
V3	Browsing / Browse3	912	*br3gt.xml*
V4	Browsing / Browse4	1140	*br4gt.xml*
V5	Browsing / Browse_WhileWaiting1	792	*bww1gt.xml*
V6	Browsing / Browse_WhileWaiting2	1896	*bww2gt.xml*
V7	Fighting / Fight_RunAway1	552	*fra1gt.xml*
V8	Fighting / Fight_RunAway2	552	*fra2gt.xml*
V9	Fighting / Fight_OneManDown (1(*), 2, 3)	960	*fomdgt1.xml*(*), *fomdgt2.xml*, *fomdgt3.xml*
V10	Fighting / Fight_Chase	432	*fcgt.xml*
V11	Groups_meeting / Meet_WalkTogether1	708	*mwt1gt.xml*
V12	Groups_meeting / Meet_WalkTogether2	828	*mwt2.gt.xml*
V13	Groups_meeting / Meet_WalkSplit	624	*mws1gt.xml*
V14	Groups_meeting / Meet_Split_3rdGuy	924	*ms3ggt.xml*
V15	Groups_meeting / Meet_Crowd	492	*mc1gt.xml*
V16	Leaving_bags / LeftBag	1440	*lb1gt.xml*
V17	Leaving_bags / LeftBag_atChair	1116	*lb2gt.xml*
V18	Leaving_bags / LeftBag_BehindChair	1068	*lbbcgt.xml*
V19	Leaving_bags / LeftBox	864	*lbgt.xml*
V20	Leaving_bags / LeftBag_PickedUp	1356	*lbpugt.xml*
V21	Rest / Rest_InChair	1008	*ricgt.xml*
V22	Rest / Rest_SlumpOnFloor	912	*rsfgt.xml*
V23	Rest / Rest_WiggleOnFloor	1189	*rwgt.xml*
V24	Rest / Rest_FallOnFloor	1008	*rffgt.xml*
V25	Walking / Walk1	612	*wk1gt.xml*
V26	Walking / Walk2	1056	*wk2gt.xml*
V27	Walking / Walk3	1380	*wk3gt.xml*

(*) *fomdgt1.xml* is selected for '*Fight_OneManDown*' videoclip

testing process as one of chosen instances. In addition, one should consider that 'Rest_WiggleOnFloor' videoclip have normally 1296 frames, but GT XML file is defined only with 1189 frames. This situation is represented in Table 5.1. Also, all of 27 GT XML files are used totally in our performance testing processes [17].

5.2 Experimental Results

In this book, we use some experimental results from our previous study in 2011 which are published in journal article as a part of the study of Karasulu and Korukoglu [17]. In addition, much of the essential material in this book is based on Bahadir Karasulu's Ph.D. dissertation published in 2010 [123]. The ViCamPEv software was designed by us so that it works as a real-time ATE and/or SATE. In our study, we compared the object D&T algorithm implementations with each other to find their accuracies on small videoclips from CAVIAR database's first dataset/scenario. Furthermore, our testing process is in real-time. The end-user may change or control relevant object D&T method and its parameters through testing process. Thence, the performance results are obtained in real-time. However, they are recorded in video-time. Therefore, the results and their plots are based on videoclip's frames. For all selected testing videos, the performance tests are made with manually predefined same default parameter settings of relevant object D&T method. While video sequence is playing, these default parameter settings can be changed interactively by end-user via GUI. The algorithms of these object D&T methods are used in implementations. They are purely like their original form. The experimental tests are executed over 10 trials by following parameters with each one of the object D&T methods. For BS method (with its variants), the tracking object ratio and keyframe, running average alpha (RAA), binarization threshold are D&T parameters. The Table 5.2 shows the BS method's variants default D&T parameter setting values on GUI [17].

For CMS method, the almost gray's threshold (S_{min}), bright pixels' threshold (V_{Max}), and almost black's threshold (V_{min}) are D&T parameters. In addition, their default parameter setting values are 50, 20, 20, respectively. In our application cvCamShift function of OpenCV is used. Its termination criterion is defined by programmatically. Thus, its epsilon value is one and its maximum iteration value is 10. For Sparse OF method, motion window size, maximum count, minimum distance, quality, and, its maximum iteration and epsilon parameters for termination criterion are D&T parameters, respectively. For Dense OF method, D&T parameters

Table 5.2 Default D&T parameter setting values of BS method's variants [17, 123]

Parameter name	Videomode1	Videomode2	Videomode3
RAA	0.055	0.055	0.055
Threshold	65	30	65
Tracking key frame	25	25	2
Tracking object ratio	0.125	0.125	0.125

Table 5.3 Default parameter setting values of the Sparse OF and Dense OF methods [17, 123]

Parameter name	Lucas-Kanade (Sparse) OF	Horn-Schunck (Dense) OF
Term. criteria max. iteration	20	20
Term. criteria epsilon	3 (i.e., 0.03)	3 (i.e., 0.03)
OF motion window size	8	Not available
OF maximum count	300	Not available
OF minimum distance	8	Not available
OF quality	1 (i.e., 0.01)	Not available

are maximum iteration and epsilon which are same as Sparse OF parameters, but other parameters of Sparse OF method are not available for Dense OF method. The default parameter setting values of Dense OF and Sparse OF methods on GUI are shown in the Table 5.3, respectively. In Table 5.3, some parameters have values shown in parentheses are normalized automatically in range between 0 and 100 by our application [17, 118].

In our experiments, all 27 video sequences of CAVIAR database's first dataset (i.e., scenario) were tested using related above mentioned parameters. We have obtained overall results for each one of the videos and each one of appropriate performance metrics over all of four above-mentioned object D&T methods through testing process. All overall results are obtained by using our system (i.e., ViCamPEv) as ATE [17].

5.2.1 Qualitative Results

In this section, some example snapshots of the frames of given videoclip used in this study are shown for understanding the importance of qualitative performance results for given D&T methods. The snapshots are taken from the *LeftBox* videoclip of CAVIAR database's first scenario [46]. In addition, these snapshots were taken while videoclip was playing by ViCamPEv software. However, the performance was measured in real-time by ViCamPEv software [17, 118]. As shown in Fig. 5.1, relevant object D&T algorithm is in action and tracks at least one object, meanwhile the performance measurement process continues. Thence, it is plotted by system in real-time. As it can be seen from the ViCamPEv software's GUI main screen, bounding boxes of GTOs are blue boxes with yellow numbers and bounding boxes of DTOs are red boxes with cyan numbers [17]. The Fig. 5.1 involves the output image of frame #39 of *LeftBox* videoclip. In Fig. 5.1a, BS method is in action. In Fig. 5.1b, CMS method is in action. In Fig. 5.1c, Dense OF method is in action. In Fig. 5.1d, Sparse OF method is in action.

One can see from Fig. 5.1 that all object D&T methods are applied on the same frame of the same videoclip. There are numerous pixels in the DT algorithm result object(s) (i.e., DTOs) and/or GT object(s) (i.e., GTOs) bounding box areas. In this

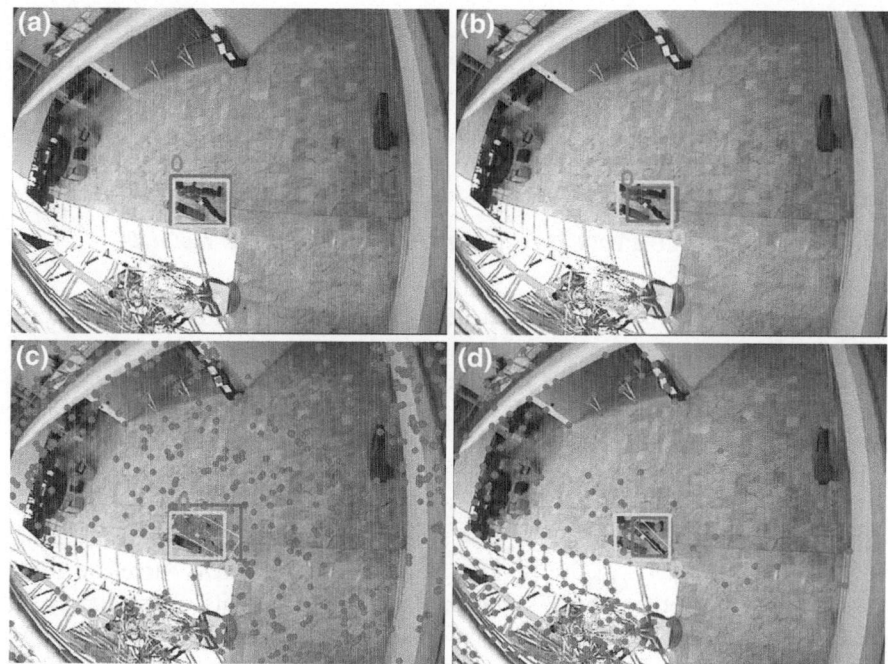

Fig. 5.1 The qualitative performance of object D&T algorithms while in action. **a** Output image obtained by using BS method. **b** Output image obtained by using CMS method. **c** Output image obtained by using Dense OF method. **d** Output image obtained by using Sparse OF method [17]

scope, one can appreciate these qualitative results via overlap ratio between bounding boxes of DTOs and GTOs. The ratio is an object segmentation result. Furthermore, it is close to '1' or '100-*percent*' value while GTOs and DTOs perfectly match. The decision is made by expert via observation in this qualitative way. By the means of this qualitative way, the BS method is more successful than other methods for object segmentation and tracking. In this frame, the Dense OF and Sparse OF methods are less successful, because BS method's output DTO bounding box is a near perfect match of GTO bounding box [17].

In a given video frame, any object D&T method may obtain instantaneously better result than other methods. Thus, the obtained qualitative results may be a misleading mark in determination of overall performance result of given D&T method. The overall performance results are the average of these instantaneous performance changes obtained using relevant object D&T method. Thus, the average result is either based on numerical values (i.e., quantitative way) or made by expert-human (i.e., qualitative way). By this decision approach, it is obvious which method is better than other methods. In a specified medium, the guideline and/or basic principle of choosing appropriate method for object D&T is a combination of these qualitative and quantitative results. One can determine some criteria for the best results, such as in quantitative way, convergence of any given performance metric to the value, 1, in qualitative way observing 100-*percent* overlap ratio between bounding boxes of GTOs and DTOs. First criterion shows numerical success of the given method, and the latter criterion shows qualitative success of the given method based on observation [17].

5.2.2 Performance Plots Based on the Quantitative Results

The experimental (i.e., performance) results for 16 metrics given in Chap. 4 are shown via ViCamPEv (i.e., via charting/plotting module) as video-frame based plots which have a range of values [17, 118]. This range is between *zero* and *one*. Thence, *zero* value and *one* value indicates the *worst* result and the *best* result for performance measurement, respectively. Furthermore, related plot express given metric's value alternations in video frames through related video sequence. These plots are independent from each other. They and their numerical values are used to compare the various algorithms. The meaning of this is that there are 1728 performance result plots (4 algorithms × 16 metrics × 27 videoclips) and 108 ROC curve and 108 *P* versus *R* plots (4 algorithms × 27 videoclips) for our experiments. Consequently, the ViCamPEv produce itself totally 540 plots (1 algorithm × 20 plots × 27 videoclips) for a given experiment. In addition, these 20 plots are obtained via performance menu and statistics menu of ViCamPEv software. There are 18 plots in performance menu. They are 16 metric plots, one *P* versus *R* plot and one ROC curve plot. There are 2 plots in statistics menu. They are one plot for Mean Square Error (MSE) and one plot for Probability Density Function (PDF). All of above mentioned plots are available as our supplementary materials on our website [118]. In addition, some of them are published in journal article as a part of the study of Karasulu and Korukoglu [17].

5.2.3 Overall Quantitative Results Based on the Performance

The overall performance results for videoclips of first dataset of CAVIAR database are measured for appropriate 12 metrics in our experiments. The details for videoclips of CAVIAR's first dataset are presented in Table 5.1 as well. These performance metrics are OCA, PBP, PBR, ATP, ATR, ABP, ABR, AF, PA, SFDA, STDA, and ATA. Their details are given in Chap. 4 of this book. Their values are given for related videoclips from Table 5.4 through Table 5.12. These values are taken from the study of Karasulu and Korukoglu [17]. In addition, the overall performance results of videoclips are shown from V1 to V3 in Table 5.4, from V4 to V6 in Table 5.5, from V7 to V9 in Table 5.6, from V10 to V12 in Table 5.7, from V13 to V15 in Table 5.8, from V16 to V18 in Table 5.9, from V19 to V21 in Table 5.10, from V22 to V24 in Table 5.11, and from V25 to V27 in Table 5.12, respectively.

Table 5.4 Overall performance results from V1 to V3 videoclips of CAVIAR [17, 123]

Method	BS (Videomode1)			CMS			Dense OF			Sparse OF		
Metric video	V1	V2	V3	V1	V2	V3	V1	V2	V3	V1	V2	V3
OCA	0.87	0.76	0.73	0.65	0.96	0.94	0.36	0.46	0.44	0.12	0.3	0.18
PBP	0.68	0.82	0.24	0.19	0.14	0.28	0.17	0.12	0.09	0.69	0.59	0.65
PBR	0.62	0.74	0.45	0.54	0.55	0.7	0.4	0.3	0.41	0.2	0.27	0.1
ATP	0.43	0.89	0.32	0.54	0.43	0.67	0.44	0.31	0.36	0.51	0.19	0.44
ATR	0.26	0.48	0.36	0.18	0.57	0.18	0.11	0.17	0.16	0.06	0.06	0.09
ABP	0.28	0.73	0.05	0.23	0.25	0.3	0.2	0.17	0.19	0.28	0.13	0.32
ABR	0.15	0.33	0.0	0.08	0.33	0.09	0.05	0.09	0.09	0.03	0.03	0.05
AF	0.42	0.78	0.63	0.38	0.81	0.71	0.17	0.32	0.29	0.07	0.09	0.15
PA	0.33	0.68	0.37	0.05	0.39	0.18	0.07	0.16	0.18	0.02	0.07	0.11
SFDA	0.19	0.5	0.25	0.09	0.22	0.24	0.03	0.05	0.06	0.01	0.03	0.04
STDA	0.08	0.24	0.09	0.03	0.1	0.11	0.01	0.02	0.03	0.0	0.01	0.02
ATA	0.08	0.27	0.06	0.04	0.1	0.12	0.02	0.03	0.04	0.01	0.01	0.03

Table 5.5 Overall performance results from V4 to V6 videoclips of CAVIAR [17, 123]

Method	BS (Videomode1)			CMS			Dense OF			Sparse OF		
Metric video	V4	V5	V6	V4	V5	V6	V4	V5	V6	V4	V5	V6
OCA	0.32	0.51	0.29	0.98	0.76	0.56	0.44	0.37	0.18	0.11	0.24	0.0
PBP	0.69	0.85	0.47	0.06	0.05	0.15	0.07	0.07	0.05	0.47	0.67	0.0
PBR	0.36	0.5	0.66	0.43	0.36	0.92	0.39	0.27	0.4	0.25	0.02	0.0
ATP	0.42	0.21	0.26	0.19	0.04	0.46	0.3	0.16	0.08	0.5	0.01	0.0
ATR	0.37	0.14	0.9	0.46	0.01	0.09	0.2	0.05	0.04	0.09	0.1	0.0
ABP	0.3	0.18	0.0	0.1	0.01	0.13	0.15	0.07	0.04	0.34	0.0	0.0
ABR	0.17	0.01	0.0	0.26	0.0	0.05	0.11	0.01	0.02	0.06	0.0	0.0
AF	0.42	0.38	0.98	0.85	0.42	0.97	0.32	0.18	0.15	0.13	0.15	0.0
PA	0.32	0.06	0.85	0.15	0.0	0.08	0.18	0.03	0.04	0.06	0.0	0.0
SFDA	0.12	0.21	0.28	0.1	0.03	0.3	0.06	0.02	0.01	0.03	0.0	0.0
STDA	0.06	0.08	0.12	0.05	0.01	0.15	0.03	0.0	0.0	0.01	0.0	0.0
ATA	0.07	0.1	0.06	0.04	0.01	0.11	0.03	0.01	0.01	0.02	0.0	0.0

5.3 Analysis of Quantitative Performance Results

The values of the various metrics for each video are shown as given data in above mentioned tables, which are given in range between *zero* and *one*. As is the case for performance plots, *zero* value and *one* value indicates the *worst* and the *best* performance result obtained by given algorithm. Furthermore, we give in Table 5.13 some statistical values obtained over 27 videoclip for each metric, i.e., the mean and standard deviation. Thus, one can use these data to make a sensible choice. In Table 5.13, the mean and standard deviation (abbreviated as st. dev.) values for all of overall performance results from V1 to V27 videoclips are shown [17].

The average of mean values of each method can be calculated from given values of Table 5.13. Thence, the average is 0.341 for BS, 0.298 for CMS, 0.169 for Dense OF, and 0.143 for Sparse OF, respectively. In this frame, there are no any metrics more

Table 5.6 Overall performance results from V7 to V9 videoclips of CAVIAR [17, 123]

Method	BS (Videomode1)			CMS			Dense OF			Sparse OF		
Metric video	V7	V8	V9	V7	V8	V9	V7	V8	V9	V7	V8	V9
OCA	0.9	0.52	0.76	0.68	0.64	0.7	0.43	0.35	0.48	0.12	0.2	0.4
PBP	0.36	0.77	0.56	0.23	0.32	0.52	0.14	0.25	0.18	0.69	0.83	0.7
PBR	0.46	0.41	0.66	0.56	0.66	0.93	0.32	0.38	0.4	0.07	0.27	0.22
ATP	0.24	0.48	0.25	0.54	0.74	0.64	0.51	0.44	0.46	0.53	0.45	0.27
ATR	0.12	0.23	0.23	0.26	0.19	0.1	0.19	0.09	0.21	0.07	0.09	0.11
ABP	0.22	0.32	0.13	0.27	0.28	0.38	0.27	0.26	0.22	0.39	0.33	0.17
ABR	0.05	0.14	0.03	0.08	0.04	0.04	0.07	0.04	0.13	0.02	0.05	0.07
AF	0.2	0.27	0.33	0.32	0.39	0.34	0.22	0.17	0.26	0.08	0.11	0.13
PA	0.06	0.19	0.19	0.08	0.16	0.07	0.05	0.07	0.12	0.01	0.07	0.05
SFDA	0.09	0.14	0.14	0.12	0.11	0.08	0.06	0.06	0.06	0.02	0.03	0.02
STDA	0.04	0.05	0.06	0.04	0.04	0.03	0.02	0.02	0.02	0.0	0.01	0.01
ATA	0.05	0.07	0.05	0.06	0.05	0.05	0.03	0.03	0.04	0.01	0.02	0.02

Table 5.7 Overall performance results from V10 to V12 videoclips of CAVIAR [17, 123]

Method	BS (Videomode1)			CMS			Dense OF			Sparse OF		
Metric video	V10	V11	V12	V10	V11	V12	V10	V11	V12	V10	V11	V12
OCA	0.66	0.42	0.8	0.44	0.63	0.73	0.28	0.27	0.35	0.26	0.02	0.14
PBP	0.61	0.71	0.46	0.2	0.24	0.13	0.27	0.11	0.1	0.84	0.14	0.59
PBR	0.38	0.68	0.53	0.48	0.87	0.44	0.37	0.34	0.37	0.12	0.08	0.15
ATP	0.41	0.51	0.31	0.65	0.42	0.24	0.56	0.19	0.26	0.41	0.2	0.28
ATR	0.18	0.23	0.13	0.16	0.03	0.16	0.1	0.04	0.08	0.08	0.0	0.03
ABP	0.37	0.47	0.15	0.25	0.15	0.11	0.29	0.07	0.14	0.23	0.08	0.2
ABR	0.12	0.08	0.06	0.06	0.0	0.11	0.03	0.0	0.04	0.04	0.0	0.01
AF	0.18	0.36	0.37	0.19	0.41	0.23	0.1	0.15	0.16	0.08	0.01	0.07
PA	0.0	0.23	0.17	0.06	0.24	0.13	0.02	0.04	0.07	0.0	0.0	0.03
SFDA	0.08	0.28	0.11	0.04	0.16	0.05	0.02	0.04	0.03	0.02	0.0	0.01
STDA	0.03	0.11	0.05	0.01	0.05	0.02	0.01	0.01	0.01	0.01	0.0	0.0
ATA	0.04	0.13	0.05	0.03	0.06	0.02	0.02	0.02	0.02	0.02	0.0	0.01

Table 5.8 Overall performance results from V13 to V15 videoclips of CAVIAR [17, 123]

Method	BS (Videomode1)			CMS			Dense OF			Sparse OF		
Metric video	V13	V14	V15	V13	V14	V15	V13	V14	V15	V13	V14	V15
OCA	0.67	0.6	0.41	0.6	0.67	0.58	0.25	0.33	0.25	0.07	0.06	0.08
PBP	0.56	0.61	0.55	0.19	0.2	0.3	0.19	0.12	0.31	0.73	0.44	0.45
PBR	0.49	0.62	0.63	0.62	0.72	0.99	0.34	0.39	0.56	0.15	0.03	0.18
ATP	0.32	0.58	0.52	0.57	0.61	0.59	0.36	0.32	0.62	0.14	0.43	0.8
ATR	0.11	0.17	0.18	0.18	0.09	0.06	0.04	0.09	0.1	0.02	0.03	0.06
ABP	0.3	0.47	0.54	0.17	0.22	0.34	0.2	0.15	0.33	0.09	0.3	0.37
ABR	0.03	0.04	0.01	0.11	0.01	0.0	0.0	0.0	0.0	0.0	0.0	0.0
AF	0.23	0.34	0.17	0.22	0.39	0.2	0.07	0.15	0.09	0.02	0.04	0.05
PA	0.15	0.27	0.11	0.02	0.07	0.15	0.02	0.08	0.06	0.0	0.03	0.03
SFDA	0.06	0.22	0.11	0.07	0.1	0.08	0.01	0.02	0.04	0.0	0.0	0.01
STDA	0.03	0.09	0.05	0.03	0.04	0.03	0.0	0.01	0.01	0.0	0.0	0.0
ATA	0.03	0.11	0.06	0.04	0.05	0.05	0.01	0.01	0.03	0.0	0.0	0.01

Table 5.9 Overall performance results from V16 to V18 videoclips of CAVIAR [17, 123]

Method	BS (Videomode1)			CMS			Dense OF			Sparse OF		
Metric video	V16	V17	V18	V16	V17	V18	V16	V17	V18	V16	V17	V18
OCA	0.78	0.78	0.8	0.78	0.77	0.87	0.41	0.43	0.46	0.13	0.16	0.16
PBP	0.61	0.41	0.53	0.23	0.15	0.27	0.16	0.11	0.13	0.6	0.51	0.47
PBR	0.45	0.4	0.57	0.35	0.59	0.69	0.31	0.38	0.44	0.1	0.1	0.13
ATP	0.54	0.31	0.47	0.54	0.57	0.47	0.42	0.35	0.44	0.42	0.31	0.37
ATR	0.39	0.22	0.24	0.17	0.23	0.24	0.15	0.16	0.16	0.06	0.04	0.09
ABP	0.46	0.16	0.34	0.23	0.26	0.17	0.21	0.16	0.21	0.25	0.2	0.27
ABR	0.25	0.07	0.14	0.13	0.05	0.12	0.08	0.07	0.06	0.03	0.02	0.02
AF	0.46	0.49	0.43	0.34	0.46	0.56	0.2	0.23	0.26	0.08	0.06	0.12
PA	0.31	0.19	0.35	0.17	0.21	0.27	0.08	0.11	0.11	0.03	0.04	0.05
SFDA	0.22	0.1	0.26	0.13	0.11	0.11	0.05	0.03	0.05	0.02	0.01	0.02
STDA	0.1	0.04	0.12	0.05	0.04	0.05	0.02	0.01	0.02	0.0	0.0	0.0
ATA	0.11	0.04	0.13	0.07	0.05	0.06	0.03	0.02	0.03	0.01	0.01	0.01

Table 5.10 Overall performance results from V19 to V21 videoclips of CAVIAR [17, 123]

Method	BS (Videomode1)			CMS			Dense OF			Sparse OF		
Metric video	V19	V20	V21	V19	V20	V21	V19	V20	V21	V19	V20	V21
OCA	0.91	0.77	0.37	0.79	0.87	0.88	0.39	0.45	0.42	0.58	0.2	0.19
PBP	0.56	0.36	0.79	0.45	0.21	0.21	0.15	0.1	0.16	0.7	0.6	0.65
PBR	0.63	0.39	0.64	0.57	0.69	0.61	0.38	0.43	0.48	0.17	0.15	0.21
ATP	0.7	0.33	0.67	0.65	0.58	0.56	0.46	0.35	0.42	0.14	0.45	0.31
ATR	0.29	0.37	0.28	0.39	0.41	0.14	0.12	0.2	0.15	0.08	0.1	0.11
ABP	0.53	0.03	0.4	0.47	0.33	0.24	0.21	0.2	0.21	0.09	0.31	0.19
ABR	0.18	0.03	0.1	0.13	0.22	0.02	0.04	0.08	0.05	0.02	0.05	0.02
AF	0.56	0.56	0.32	0.55	0.54	0.59	0.21	0.3	0.24	0.11	0.14	0.14
PA	0.44	0.51	0.19	0.12	0.31	0.06	0.07	0.14	0.1	0.02	0.1	0.05
SFDA	0.36	0.23	0.14	0.14	0.25	0.17	0.05	0.06	0.05	0.04	0.04	0.01
STDA	0.16	0.09	0.06	0.05	0.1	0.08	0.02	0.02	0.02	0.01	0.02	0.0
ATA	0.17	0.06	0.09	0.07	0.11	0.09	0.03	0.04	0.03	0.02	0.03	0.01

Table 5.11 Overall performance results from V22 to V24 videoclips of CAVIAR [17, 123]

Method	BS (Videomode1)			CMS			Dense OF			Sparse OF		
Metric video	V22	V23	V24	V22	V23	V24	V22	V23	V24	V22	V23	V24
OCA	0.87	0.7	0.64	0.9	0.89	0.93	0.49	0.36	0.45	0.32	0.09	0.17
PBP	0.71	0.6	0.29	0.72	0.16	0.27	0.16	0.11	0.11	0.42	0.46	0.67
PBR	0.75	0.78	0.36	0.67	0.75	0.88	0.5	0.44	0.32	0.16	0.12	0.08
ATP	0.58	0.37	0.24	0.4	0.58	0.64	0.39	0.28	0.27	0.22	0.54	0.52
ATR	0.4	0.18	0.4	0.22	0.35	0.14	0.18	0.1	0.14	0.1	0.05	0.09
ABP	0.35	0.07	0.05	0.24	0.18	0.25	0.21	0.16	0.16	0.15	0.33	0.41
ABR	0.22	0.0	0.04	0.11	0.24	0.07	0.1	0.02	0.07	0.06	0.0	0.06
AF	0.64	0.55	0.54	0.67	0.67	0.64	0.31	0.19	0.24	0.18	0.08	0.13
PA	0.6	0.44	0.32	0.12	0.28	0.48	0.17	0.09	0.12	0.1	0.05	0.1
SFDA	0.46	0.41	0.17	0.11	0.16	0.24	0.06	0.04	0.04	0.02	0.02	0.04
STDA	0.2	0.14	0.06	0.04	0.07	0.1	0.02	0.01	0.01	0.01	0.0	0.02
ATA	0.19	0.12	0.04	0.05	0.07	0.11	0.03	0.02	0.02	0.01	0.01	0.04

Table 5.12 Overall performance results from V25 to V27 videoclips of CAVIAR [17, 123]

Method	BS (Videomode1)			CMS			Dense OF			Sparse OF		
Metric video	V25	V26	V27	V25	V26	V27	V25	V26	V27	V25	V26	V27
OCA	0.5	0.74	0.59	0.55	0.53	0.96	0.28	0.23	0.46	0.09	0.15	0.15
PBP	0.86	0.34	0.77	0.17	0.18	0.11	0.26	0.21	0.09	0.84	0.61	0.59
PBR	0.55	0.16	0.93	0.57	0.46	0.6	0.54	0.37	0.4	0.18	0.16	0.2
ATP	0.76	0.45	0.9	0.56	0.5	0.35	0.57	0.31	0.33	0.47	0.01	0.44
ATR	0.17	0.31	0.3	0.29	0.34	0.24	0.09	0.01	0.29	0.05	0.0	0.12
ABP	0.6	0.4	0.65	0.21	0.22	0.12	0.29	0.13	0.18	0.21	0.01	0.3
ABR	0.0	0.15	0.24	0.0	0.09	0.14	0.0	0.0	0.15	0.0	0.0	0.05
AF	0.26	0.26	0.8	0.27	0.27	0.79	0.12	0.1	0.45	0.05	0.06	0.17
PA	0.05	0.11	0.75	0.0	0.07	0.41	0.03	0.02	0.28	0.0	0.0	0.12
SFDA	0.13	0.09	0.61	0.06	0.04	0.17	0.02	0.02	0.09	0.0	0.0	0.04
STDA	0.06	0.03	0.3	0.02	0.02	0.08	0.01	0.0	0.04	0.0	0.0	0.02
ATA	0.08	0.04	0.32	0.04	0.03	0.07	0.02	0.01	0.05	0.0	0.0	0.03

Table 5.13 The mean and standard deviation (abbreviated as st. dev.) values for all of overall performance results from V1 to V27 videoclips of CAVIAR [17, 123]

Method	BS (Videomode1)		CMS		Dense OF		Sparse OF	
Metric	Mean	St. Dev.	Mean	St. Dev.	Mean	St. Dev.	Mean	St. Dev.
OCA	0.65	0.18	0.75	0.15	0.37	0.08	0.17	0.12
PBP	0.58	0.17	0.24	0.14	0.15	0.06	0.58	0.19
PBR	0.55	0.16	0.64	0.17	0.39	0.06	0.14	0.07
ATP	0.46	0.19	0.51	0.15	0.37	0.12	0.35	0.19
ATR	0.28	0.15	0.22	0.13	0.13	0.06	0.07	0.03
ABP	0.32	0.2	0.23	0.09	0.19	0.06	0.22	0.12
ABR	0.1	0.09	0.1	0.08	0.05	0.04	0.02	0.02
AF	0.44	0.2	0.49	0.21	0.21	0.08	0.09	0.04
PA	0.31	0.22	0.16	0.12	0.09	0.06	0.04	0.03
SFDA	0.22	0.14	0.13	0.07	0.04	0.01	0.02	0.01
STDA	0.09	0.06	0.05	0.03	0.02	0.0	0.01	0.0
ATA	0.1	0.07	0.06	0.02	0.02	0.01	0.01	0.01

representative or comprehensive of algorithmic performance than another because of their independency for measurement. However, they are considered as a set of performance results for final evaluation. It is seen from all of these values from Table 5.4 through Table 5.13, the BS method performance is preferable than the others because of its high values [17].

5.3.1 Statistical Analysis

In our statistical analysis, we used Minitab statistical program and its Box-Cox type power transformation to analyze our data of performance results with a general

Table 5.14 Analysis of variance of overall performance results for all aforementioned methods [17]

Source	DF	Adj. SS	Adj. MS	F	P_v
METHODS	3	9.34014	3.11338	399.76	0.000
VIDEOS(METHODS)	104	7.75721	0.07459	9.58	0.000
METRICS	11	29.34296	2.66754	342.51	0.000
METHODS*METRICS	33	4.60966	0.13969	17.94	0.000
Error	1144	8.90966	0.00779		
Total	1295	59.95964			

linear model. In this analysis, we have considered the skewness of our data. The resulting transformation is $Y^{0.30547}$. Then, we assumed split plot analysis with all aforementioned methods as the whole plot factor and videoclips as the split plot factor. For the results of the calculations, the analysis of variance (ANOVA) associated with the split plot design displayed in Table 5.14. In this table, the degrees of freedom, adjusted sum of squares, adjusted mean square, F-statistic, and Probability-value are abbreviated as DF, Adj. SS, Adj. MS, F, and P_v, respectively.

Consequently, one can see that from the Table 5.14, all of the probabilities are less than 0.01. Furthermore, one can conclude that there are differences among the methods, metrics, and the interaction between methods and metrics is also important. For Table 5.14 values, R-square is 85.14%. In Fig. 5.2, the residual plots of ANOVA are shown together. In Fig. 5.3, the main effects of the factors are shown. These plots in Figs. 5.2 and 5.3 are produced by Minitab program [17].

It is seen from the Fig. 5.3, the BS method performance is preferable than the others. For all above mentioned methods, the means of performance results based

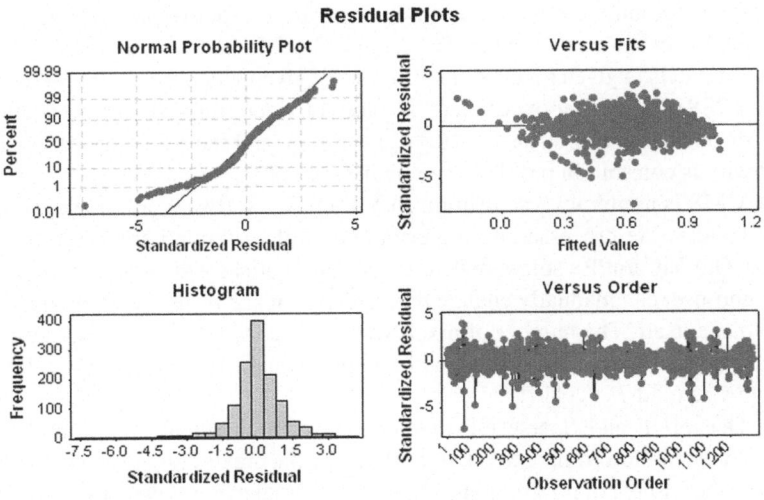

Fig. 5.2 The residual plots of ANOVA [17]

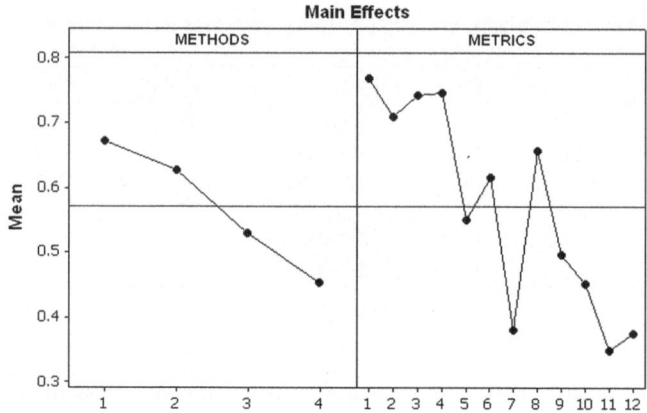

Fig. 5.3 The main effects [17]

on metrics and videoclips are ordered such as BS, CMS, Dense OF, and Sparse OF, respectively. In Fig. 5.3, the subplot of mean of methods shows this order obtained by our statistical analysis, where **1** is BS, **2** is CMS, **3** is Dense OF and **4** is Sparse OF. Also, in the same figure, the subplot of mean of metrics shows the total order of overall results based on each metric's value.

5.3.2 Algorithmic Analysis

In this book, BS method's '*videomodel*' variant's algorithm uses *pure* background averaging. Therefore, the classification is just a thresholded difference for each pixel. Also, the background model update of BS adapts just one or two parameters. Thus, its time complexity can be defined as $T_{\text{BackAve}} = O(1)$. In addition, let the F_{Size} be the number of pixels in given image or picture size of given video frame. It is determined as 384×288 pixels in our experiment, because of video frame size of first dataset of CAVIAR database. Thus, $T_{\text{BS}} = O(F_{\text{Size}}) \approx O(1)$, and the BS computational time complexity is constant in problem size (and F_{Size}) [17].

The CMS is an iterative algorithm. In ViCamPEv software, all pixels inside the search window are processed during each one of algorithmic iteration of the CMS method. Our ViCamPEv software determines automatically the search window size, or, the end-user can manually change this size, thus it can be less than or equal to the given image itself. The number of pixels in the search window is bounded by F_{Size}. Thus, $T_{\text{CMS}} = O(F_{\text{Size}})$, and the CMS computational time complexity is linear in problem size (and F_{Size}) [17].

For Dense OF and Sparse OF method, the computational time complexity is dependent on motion complexity. Let the H_{Max} be the maximum motion velocity. Let the R_{F} be the number of flow regions. These methods take into consideration the entire video frame's image. Let N_{Point} be the number of features (i.e., points). The algorithm

Table 5.15 Computational time of relevant object D&T methods used in our ViCamPEv software [17]

Algorithm of relevant method	Color space	Processing speed (frames per second) (fps)	Computational time (milliseconds per frame) (ms)	Algorithm's total computational complexity
BS	RGB and Grayscale	25	35	$T_{BS} = O(1)$
CMS	HSV or HSI	25	10	$T_{CMS} = O(F_{Size})$
Dense OF	RGB	25	105	$T_{DenseOF} = O(F_{Size} \times N_{Point} \times H_{Max}/R_F)$
Sparse OF	RGB	25	20	$T_{SparseOF} = O(F_{Size} \times N_{Point} \times H_{Max})$

of Dense OF method divides the image into R_F regions. It deals frequently to detect more features than Sparse OF for given video. For Sparse OF, the R_F is one. In our software, a modified version of KLT (Kanade-Lucas-Tomasi) feature tracker is used by Sparse OF method [104]. Thence, one can calculate the time complexity in terms of image size (i.e., F_{Size}), number of features (i.e., N_{Point}) and maximum motion velocity (i.e., H_{Max}). Therefore, $T_{DenseOF} = O(F_{Size} \times N_{Point} \times H_{Max}/R_F)$ is for Dense OF and $T_{SparseOF} = O(F_{Size} \times N_{Point} \times H_{Max})$ is for Sparse OF, and the Dense OF and Sparse OF computational time complexity is linear in problem size (i.e., F_{Size}, N_{Point} and H_{Max}) [17].

Relevant object D&T method of our software processes each video frame in terms of milliseconds (i.e., ms). In the experiments, the BS, CMS, Dense OF, and Sparse OF method has computational time for each video frame which is approximately 35, 10, 105, and 20 ms, respectively. These computational times may be changing according to relevant algorithmic parameters and video clip. Their change range is between 10 ms (i.e., minimum in Table 5.15) and 120 ms (i.e., maximum in Table 5.15). The approximate values of these computational times of above mentioned algorithms are given in Table 5.15. Our application calculates these values automatically for each frame of given video. In addition, these values involve pre-computation and per-iteration times as well. For more details, the reader may refer to the study of Karasulu and Korukoglu [17].

Chapter 6
Conclusion

Abstract This chapter concludes the book, also it involves a summary of the study. Therefore, it declares some contributions of given study. In addition, this chapter suggests to readers or researchers in computer vision and multimedia research area that the ViCamPEv software is useful for image and video processing, multimedia content, and information retrieval as well.

Keywords ViCamPEv · Ground-truth · Performance evaluation

6.1 Main Contribution

The main contribution of our study explained in this book is to develop real-time performance measurement and evaluation software for testing together the commonly implemented algorithms of object D&T methods employed in the same platform. Thence, these algorithms are based on BS, CMS, Dense OF, and Sparse OF methods.

First contribution of our study is software stability and flexibility for comparison of different methods by using the same metrics in real time. Second contribution of our study is human-understandable representation of XML GT file for end user. The ViCamPEv [17, 118] has an integrated XML GT file loading/viewing module. It supports above-mentioned representation. Thence, end users can select or deselect easily from GT data either specified object(s) or all of them for object D&T process. Another valuable contribution of this book is to present a comprehensive literature survey of above-mentioned video object D&T methods.

6.2 Suggestion

The researchers can prefer ViCamPEv [17, 118] because of interaction capabilities of the program. The kind of interaction can have negative or positive effects on the performance in real time. While the testing process continues, end user can change feature points, bounding boxes of object(s) or parameters of relevant methods and/or add a morphological operation or a filter on to current playing frame simultaneously. The performance of relevant methods is measured by program in a full-automatic way. Therefore, the performance reporting module and/or charting/plotting module of ViCamPEv gives an opportunity to end user to exchange their results with other end users. The ViCamPEv software is useful for video processing, information retrieval, and multimedia content retrieval and indexing research areas.

References

1. Remagnino P, Jones GA, Paragios N, Regazzoni CS (eds) (2002) Video-based surveillance systems: computer vision and distributed processing. Kluwer Academic, Dordrecht. ISBN / ISSN 0-7923-7632-3
2. Foresti GL, Regazzoni CS, Varshney PK (2003) Multisensor surveillance systems: the fusion perspective. Kluwer Academic, Dordrecht. ISBN/ISNN 1-4020-7492-1
3. Erdem CE, Ernst F, Redert A, Hendriks E (2005) Temporal stabilization of video object tracking for 3D-TV applications. Signal Process Image Commun 20(2):151–167. doi: 10.1016/j.image.2004.10.005
4. Liu C, Yuen PC, Qiu G (2009) Object motion detection using information theoretic spatio-temporal saliency. Pattern Recognit 42(11):2897–2906. doi:10.1016/j.patcog.2009.02.002
5. Zhong Q, Qingqing Z, Tengfei G (2012) Moving object tracking based on codebook and particle filter. Procedia Eng 29:174–178. doi:10.1016/j.proeng.2011.12.690
6. Brox T, Bruhn A, Weickert J (2006) Variational motion segmentation with level sets. In: European conference on computer vision, pp 471–483
7. Yokoyama M, Poggio T (2005) A contour-based moving object detection and tracking. In: IEEE International workshop on visual surveillance and performance evaluation of tracking and surveillance, pp 271–276
8. Fang W, Chan KL (2006) Using statistical shape priors in geodesic active contours for robust object detection. In: International conference on pattern recognition, pp 304–307
9. Stocker AA (2002) An improved 2d optical flow sensor for motion segmentation. In: Proceedings of IEEE international symposium on circuits and systems, vol 2, pp 332–335
10. Singh SPN, Csonka PJ, Waldron KJ (2006) Optical flow aided motion estimation for legged locomotion. In: IEEE international conference on intelligent robots and systems, pp 1738–1743
11. Mittal A, Paragios N (2004) Motion-based background subtraction using adaptive kernel density estimation. In: Proceedings of IEEE computer society conference on computer vision and pattern recognition, pp 302–309
12. Stauffer C, Grimson WEL (1999) Adaptive background mixture models for real-time tracking. In: Proceedings of IEEE computer society conference on computer vision and pattern recognition (CVPR), pp 246–252
13. Zivkovic Z, van der Heijden F (2006) Efficient adaptive density estimation per image pixel for the task of background subtraction. Pattern Recognit Lett 27(7):773–780
14. Yu T, Zhang C, Cohen M, Rui Y, Wu Y (2007) Monocular video foreground/background segmentation by tracking spatial-color Gaussian mixture models. In: Proceedings of the IEEE workshop on motion and video computing, pp 27–32
15. Elgammal A, Harwood D, Davis LS (2000) Non-parametric model for background subtraction. In: Proceedings of the 6th european conference on computer vision, pp 751–767

16. Liu Y, Yao H, Gao W, Chen X, Zhao D (2006) Nonparametric background generation. In: International conference on pattern recognition, pp 916–919
17. Karasulu B, Korukoglu S (2011) A software for performance evaluation and comparison of people detection and tracking methods in video processing. Multimedia Tool Appl 55(3):677–723. doi:10.1007/s11042-010-0591-2
18. Huang K, Wang L, Tan T, Maybank S (2008) A real-time object detecting and tracking system for outdoor night surveillance. Pattern Recognit 41(1):432–444. doi: 10.1016/j.patcog.2007.05.017
19. Crandall D, Luo J (2004) Robust color object detection using spatial-color joint probability functions. In: Proceedings of CVPR, pp 379–385
20. Weng J, Ahuja J, Huang TS (1992) Matching two perspective views. Pattern Anal Mach Intel 14(8):806–825
21. Krattenthaler W, Mayer KJ, Zeiler M (1994) Point correlation: a reduced const template matching technique. In: ICIP, pp 208–212
22. Harris CG, Stephens M (1988) A combined corner and edge detector. In: Fourth Alvey vision conference, Manchester, pp 147–151
23. Wren CR, Azarbayejani A, Darrell T, Pentland AP (1997) Pfinder: real-time tracking of the human body. IEEE Trans Pattern Anal Mach Intel 19(7):780–785. doi:10.1109/34.598236
24. Li L, Huang W, Gu IY-H, Tian Q (2004) Statistical modeling of complex backgrounds for foreground object detection. IEEE Trans Image Process 13(11):1459–1472
25. Jain AK, Zhong Y, Lakshmanan S (1996) Object matching using deformable templates. Pattern Anal Mach Intel 18(3):267–278
26. Sclaroff S, Liu L (2001) Deformable shape detection and description via model based region grouping. Pattern Anal Mach Intel 23(5):475–489
27. Lei B, Xu L-Q (2006) Real-time outdoor video surveillance with robust foreground extraction and object tracking via multi-state transition management. Pattern Recognit Lett 27(15):1816–1825. doi:10.1016/j.patrec.2006.02.017
28. Xu LQ, Puig P (2005) A hybrid blob- and appearance-based framework for multi-object tracking through complex occlusions. In: Proceedings of 2nd joint IEEE VS-PETS workshop, Beijing, pp 73–80
29. Brdiczka O, Yuen P, Zaidenberg S, Reignier P, Crowley JL (2006) Automatic acquisition of context models and its application to video surveillance. In: 18th international conference on pattern recognition (ICPR'06), Hong Kong, Aug 2006, pp 1175–1178
30. Yilmaz A, Javed O, Shah M (2006) Object tracking: a survey. ACM Comput Surv 38(4):13–45. doi:10.1145/1177352.1177355
31. Torralba A, Murphy KP, Freeman WT, Rubin MA (2003) Context-based vision system for place and object recognition. In: Proceedings of IEEE international conference on computer vision (ICCV), Nice, France
32. Carmona EJ, Martínez-Cantos J, Mira J (2008) A new video segmentation method of moving objects based on blob-level knowledge. Pattern Recognit Lett 29(3):272–285. doi: 10.1016/j.patrec.2007.10.007
33. Haritaoglu I, Harwood D, Davis LS (2000) W^4: real-time surveillance of people and their activities. IEEE Trans Pattern Anal Mach Intel 22(8):809–830. doi: 10.1109/34.868683
34. Bradski GR (1998) Computer vision face tracking for use in a perceptual user interface. Intel Technol J Q2. http://download.intel.com/technology/itj/q21998/pdf/camshift.pdf
35. François RJA (2004) CAMSHIFT tracker design experiments with intel OpenCV and SAI. IRIS technical report IRIS-04-423, University of Southern California, Los Angeles, USA
36. Comaniciu D, Meer P (1999) Mean shift analysis and applications. In: Proceedings of IEEE international conference on computer vision (ICCV'99), Kerkyra, Greece, pp 1197–1203
37. Jodoin PM, Mignotte M (2009) Optical-flow based on an edge-avoidance procedure. Comput Vis Image Underst 113(4):511–531. doi:10.1016/j.cviu.2008.12.005

38. Pauwels K, Van Hulle MM (2009) Optic flow from unstable sequences through local velocity constancy maximization. Image Vis Comput 27(5):579–587. doi: 10.1016/j.imavis.2008.04.010 (Proceedings of the 17th British machine vision conference (BMVC 2006))

39. Kasturi R, Goldgof D, Soundararajan P, Manohar V, Garofolo J, Bowers R, Boonstra M, Korzhova V, Zhang J (2009) Framework for performance evaluation of face, text, and vehicle detection and tracking in video: data, metrics, and protocol. IEEE Trans Pattern Anal Mach Intel 31(2):319–336. doi:10.1109/TPAMI.2008.57

40. Lazarevic-McManus N, Renno JR, Makris D, Jones GA (2008) An object-based comparative methodology for motion detection based on the F-measure. Comput Vis Image Underst 111(1):74–85. doi:10.1016/j.cviu.2007.07.007 (Special issue on intelligent visual surveillance)

41. Mitsubishi MERL (2009) PEP: performance evaluation platform for object tracking methods. http://www.merl.com/projects/pep/. Accessed 01 April 2012

42. Sacan A, Ferhatosmanoglu H, Coskun H (2008) Cell track: an open-source software for cell tracking and motility analysis. Bioinformatics 24(14):1647–1649. doi: 10.1093/bioinformatics/btn247 (Advance access published on 29 May 2008)

43. Baumann A, Boltz M, Ebling J, Koenig M, Loos HS, Merkel M, Niem W, Warzelhan JK, Yu J (2008) A review and comparison of measures for automatic video surveillance systems. EURASIP J Image Video Process 2008:Article ID 824726, 30 pp. doi: 10.1155/2008/824726

44. Manohar V, Boonstra M, Korzhova V, Soundararajan P, Goldgof D, Kasturi R, Parasad S, Raju H, Bowers R, Garofolo J (2006) PETS vs. VACE evaluation programs: a comparative study. In: Proceedings of 9th IEEE international workshop on PETS, Newyork, USA, 18 June 2006, pp 1–6

45. Bashir F, Porikli F (2006) Performance evaluation of object detection and tracking systems. In: Proceedings of 9th IEEE international workshop on PETS, Newyork, USA, 18 June 2006, pp 7–14

46. CAVIAR (2009) Context aware vision using image-based active recognition. http://homepages.inf.ed.ac.uk/rbf/CAVIAR. Accessed 01 April 2012

47. VIPeR (2009) Viewpoint invariant pedestrian recognition. http://vision.soe.ucsc.edu/node/178. Accessed 01 April 2012

48. Jaynes C, Webb S, Steele RM, Xiong Q (2002) An open development environment for evaluation of video surveillance systems (ODViS). In: Proceedings of 3rd IEEE international workshop on PETS (PETS'2002), Copenhagen, Denmark, June 2002, pp 32–39

49. AVITrack (2009) Aircraft surroundings, categorised vehicles & individuals tracking for apron's activity model interpretation & check. http://www.avitrack.net. Accessed 01 April 2012

50. List T, Fisher RB (2004) CVML—an XML-based computer vision markup language. In: Proceedings of the 17th international conference on pattern recognition (ICPR 04), vol 1. Cambridge, pp 789–792. doi:10.1109/ICPR.2004.1334335 Aug 2004

51. CLEAR (2009) Classification of events, activities and relationships—evaluation campaign and workshop. http://www.clear-evaluation.org. Accessed 01 April 2012

52. CREDS (2009) Call for real-time event detection solutions (creds) for enhanced security and safety in public transportation. http://www.visiowave.com/pdf/ISAProgram/CREDS.pdf. Accessed 01 April 2012

53. PETS (2007) IEEE international workshop on performance evaluation of tracking and surveillance. http://pets2007.net. Accessed 01 April 2012

54. VACE (2009) Video analysis and content extraction. http://videorecognition.com/vt4ns/. Accessed 01 April 2012

55. Camara-Chavez G, Precioso F, Cord M, Phillip-Foliguet S, de A Araujo A (2008) An interactive video content-bawsed retrieval system. In: Proceedings of 15th international conference on systems, signals and image process (IWSSIP 2008), pp 133–136
56. Koprinska I, Carrato S (2001) Temporal video segmentation: a survey. Signal Process Image Commun 16(5):477–500. doi:10.1016/S0923-5965(00)00011-4
57. Karasulu B (2010) Review and evaluation of well-known methods for moving object detection and tracking in videos. J Aeronaut Space Technol 4(4):11–22
58. Nixon MS, Aguado AS (2001) Feature extraction and image processing. Elsevier Science Ltd., Oxford, ISBN: 0750650788
59. Sankaranarayanan AC, Veeraraghavan A, Chellappa R (2008) Object detection, tracking and recognition for multiple smart cameras. Proc IEEE 96(10):1606–1624
60. Moeslund TB (2012) Introduction to video and image processing. Undergraduate topics in computer science. Springer-Verlag, London Ltd. doi:10.1007/978-1-4471-2503-7_2
61. Wu M, Peng X (2010) Spatio-temporal context for codebook-based dynamic background subtraction. AEU Int J Electron Commun 64(8):739–747. doi:10.1016/j.aeue.2009.05.004
62. Benezeth Y, Jodoin PM, Emile B, Laurent H, Rosenberger C (2008) Review and evaluation of commonly-implemented background subtraction algorithms. In: 19th international conference on pattern recognition (ICPR 2008), pp 1–4, 8–11 Dec 2008. doi: 10.1109/ICPR.2008.4760998
63. Cheung SC, Kamath C (2004) Robust techniques for background subtraction in urban traffic video. Video communications and image processing, SPIE electronic imaging, San Jose, January, UCRL-JC-153846-ABS, UCRL-CONF-200706
64. Wand MP, Jones MC (1995) Kernel smoothing. Chapman and Hall, London
65. Wang H, Suter D (2007) A consensus-based method for tracking: modeling background scenario and foreground appearance. Pattern Recognit 40(3):1091–1105
66. Sheikh Y, Shah M (2005) Bayesian modeling of dynamic scenes for objects detection. IEEE Trans Pattern Anal Mach Intell 27:1778–1792
67. Zhong J, Sclaroff S (2003) Segmenting foreground objects from a dynamic textured background via a robust Kalman filter. In: Proceedings of IEEE international conference on computer vision, vol 1. Nice, France, pp 44–50
68. Dalley G, Migdal J, Grimson WEL (2008) Background subtraction for temporally irregular dynamic textures. In: IEEE workshop on application of computer vision, Copper Mountain, Colorado, USA, pp 1–7
69. Mandellos NA, Keramitsoglou I, Kiranoudis CT (2011) A background subtraction algorithm for detecting and tracking vehicles. Expert Syst Appl 38(3):1619–1631. doi: 10.1016/j.eswa.2010.07.083
70. Spagnolo P, Orazio TD, Leo M, Distante A (2006) Moving object segmentation by background subtraction and temporal analysis. Image Vis Comput 24(5):411–423. doi: 10.1016/j.imavis.2006.01.001
71. Zhang R, Ding J (2012) Object tracking and detecting based on adaptive background subtraction. Procedia Eng 29:1351–1355. doi:10.1016/j.proeng.2012.01.139
72. Shoushtarian B, Bez HE (2005) A practical adaptive approach for dynamic background subtraction using an invariant colour model and object tracking. Pattern Recognit Lett 26(1):5–26. doi:10.1016/j.patrec.2004.07.013
73. Magee DR (2004) Tracking multiple vehicles using foreground, background and motion models. Image Vis Comput 22(2):143–155. doi:10.1016/S0262-8856(03)00145-8
74. El Maadi A, Maldague X (2007) Outdoor infrared video surveillance: a novel dynamic technique for the subtraction of a changing background of IR images. Infrared Phys Technol 49(3):261–265. doi:10.1016/j.infrared.2006.06.015
75. Davis JW, Sharma V (2007) Background-subtraction using contour-based fusion of thermal and visible imagery. Comput Vis Image Underst 106(2–3):162–182. doi: 10.1016/j.cviu.2006.06.010

76. Comaniciu D, Meer P (2002) Mean shift: a robust approach toward feature space analysis. IEEE Trans Pattern Anal Mach Intell 24(5):603–619. doi:10.1109/34.1000236
77. Bradski G, Kaehler A (2008) Learning OpenCV: computer vision with the OpenCV library. OReilly Media, Inc. Publication, 1005 Gravenstein Highway North, Sebastopol, CA 95472, ISBN: 978-0-596-51613-0.
78. OpenCV (2012) The Open Computer Vision Library. http://sourceforge.net/projects/opencvlibrary/. Accessed 10 May 2010
79. Shan C, Tan T, Wei Y (2007) Real-time hand tracking using a mean shift embedded particle filter. Pattern Recognit 40(7):1958–1970. doi:10.1016/j.patcog.2006.12.012
80. Nummiaro K, Koller-Meier E, Van Gool LJ (2003) An adaptive color-based particle filter. Image Vis Comput 21(1):99–110. doi:10.1016/S0262-8856(02)00129-4
81. Comaniciu D, Ramesh V (2000) Mean shift and optimal prediction for efficient object tracking. In: Proceedings of IEEE conference on image process (ICIP 2000), Vancouver, Canada, vol 3, pp 70–73. doi:10.1109/ICIP.2000.899297
82. Yang C, Duraiswami R, Davis L (2005) Efficient mean-shift tracking via a new similarity measure. In: Proceedings of IEEE conference on computer vision and pattern recognition (CVPR05), vol 1. IEEE Press, Washington, pp 176–183
83. Szeliski R (2011) Computer vision: algorithms and applications, texts in computer science, 1st edn. Springer-Verlag London Limited, London
84. Karasulu B (2011) ISeeMP: a benchmark software for multithreading performance of image segmentation using clustering and thresholding techniques. In: Proceedings of 2nd international symposium on computing in science & engineering (ISCSE 2011), Gediz University, Kusadasi, Aydin, Turkey, pp 2–8
85. Li H, Ngan KN (2011) Image/video segmentation: current status, trends, and challenges. In: Ngan KN, Li H (eds) Video segmentation and its applications, Chapter 1. Springer Science + Business Media LLC, New York, pp 1–23
86. Zhou H, Wang X, Schaefer G (2011) Mean shift and its application in image segmentation, In: Kwasnicka H, Jain LC (eds) Innovations in intelligent image analysis, Chapter 13, Studies in computational intelligence 339. Springer-Verlag, Berlin, pp 291–312
87. Wang Y-H, Han C-Z (2010) PolSAR image segmentation by mean shift clustering in the tensor space. Acta Automatica Sinica 36(6):798–806. doi:10.1016/S1874-1029(09)60037-9
88. Kerminen P, Gabbouj M (1999) Image retrieval based on color matching. In: Proceedings of Finnish signal process, symposium (FINSIG-99), pp 89–93
89. Stern H, Efros B (2005) Adaptive color space switching for tracking under varying illumination. Image Vis Comput 23(3):353–364. doi:10.1016/j.imavis.2004.09.005
90. Li S-X, Chang H-X, Zhu C-F (2010) Adaptive pyramid mean shift for global real-time visual tracking. Image Vis Comput 28(3):424–437. doi:10.1016/j.imavis.2009.06.012
91. Yuan G-W, Gao Y, Xu D (2011) A moving objects tracking method based on a combination of local binary pattern texture and Hue. Procedia Eng 15:3964–3968. doi:10.1016/j.proeng.2011.08.742
92. Mazinan AH, Amir-Latifi A (2012) Applying mean shift, motion information and Kalman filtering approaches to object tracking. ISA Trans 51(3):485–497. doi:10.1016/j.isatra.2012.02.002
93. Jung K, Han JH (2004) Hybrid approach to efficient text extraction in complex color images. Pattern Recognit Lett 25(6):679–699. doi:10.1016/j.patrec.2004.01.017
94. Babu RV, Suresh S, Makur A (2010) Online adaptive radial basis function networks for robust object tracking. Comput Vis Image Underst 114(3):297–310. doi:10.1016/j.cviu.2009.10.004
95. Wang Z, Yang X, Xu Y, Yu S (2009) CamShift guided particle filter for visual tracking. Pattern Recognit Lett 30(4):407–413. doi:10.1016/j.patrec.2008.10.017
96. Yin M, Zhang J, Sun H, Gu W (2011) Multi-cue-based CamShift guided particle filter tracking. Expert Syst Appl 38(5):6313–6318. doi:10.1016/j.eswa.2010.11.111

97. González-Ortega D, Díaz-Pernas FJ, Martínez-Zarzuela M (2010) Real-time hands, face and facial features detection and tracking: Application to cognitive rehabilitation tests monitoring. J Netw Comput Appl 33(4):447–466. doi:10.1016/j.jnca.2010.02.001

98. Hu J-S, Juan C-W, Wang J-J (2008) A spatial-color mean-shift object tracking algorithm with scale and orientation estimation. Pattern Recognit Lett 29(16):2165–2173. doi: 10.1016/j.patrec.2008.08.007

99. Porikli F (2002) Automatic video object segmentation. Ph D dissertation, Electrical and Computer Engineering, Polytechnic University, Brooklyn

100. Fleet DJ, Weiss Y (2005) Optical flow estimation. In: N Paragios, Y Chen, O Faugeras (eds) Mathematical models in computer vision: the handbook, Chapter 15. Springer-Verlag, Berlin, pp 239–258

101. Horn BKP, Schunck BG (1981) Determining optical flow. Artif Intell 17(1–3):185–203. doi: 10.1016/0004-3702(81)90024-2

102. Lucas BD, Kanade T (1981) An iterative image registration technique with an application to stereo vision. In; Proceedings of seventh international joint conference on artificial intelligence, Vancouver, Canada, vol 2, pp 674–679

103. Schunck BG (1986) The image flow constraint equation. Comput Vis Graph Image Process 35(1):20–46. doi:10.1016/0734-189X(86)90124-6

104. Shi J, Tomasi C (1994) Good features to track. In: IEEE conference on computer vision and, pattern recognition (CVPR), pp 593–600. doi:10.1109/CVPR.1994.323794

105. Zheng N, Xue J (2009) Statistical learning and pattern analysis for image and video processing, Chapter 7, Advances in pattern recognition. Springer-Verlag London Limited, pp 181–216, ISBN: 978-1-84882-311-2. doi:10.1007/978-1-84882-312-9_7

106. Black MJ, Jepson AD (1996) Estimating optical flow in segmented images using variable order parametric models with local deformations. IEEE Trans Pattern Anal Mach Intell 18(10):972–986. doi:10.1109/34.541407

107. Lai S-H (2004) Computation of optical flow under non-uniform brightness variations. Pattern Recognit Lett 25(8):885–892. doi:10.1016/j.patrec.2004.02.001

108. Teng C-H, Lai S-H, Chen Y-S, Hsu W-H (2005) Accurate optical flow computation under non-uniform brightness variations. Comput Vis Image Underst 97(3):315–346. doi: 10.1016/j.cviu.2004.08.002

109. Yang D, Li J, Xiong K, Guan Z (2011) A real-time optical flow computation method used in vision based navigation control. Energy Procedia 13:3396–3402. doi: 10.1016/j.egypro.2011.11.489. Accessed 04 May 2012

110. Bruhn A, Weickert J, Schnörr C (2002) Combining the advantages of local and global optic flow methods. In: Proceedings of the 24th DAGM symposium on pattern recognition. Van Gool LJ (ed) LNCS 2449. Springer-Verlag, Berlin, pp 454–462

111. Sahba N, Tavakoli V, Ahmadian A, Abolhassani MD, Fotouhi M (2008) Hybrid local/global optical flow and spline multi-resolution analysis of myocardial motion in B-mode echocardiography images. Electron J Tech Acoust 12:1–18. http://www.ejta.org. Accessed 01 April 2012

112. Baker S, Matthews I (2004) Lucas-Kanade 20 years on: a unifying framework. Int J Comput Vis 56(3):221–255. doi:10.1023/B:VISI.0000011205.11775.fd

113. Yin J, Han Y, Hou W, Li J (2011) Detection of the mobile object with camouflage color under dynamic background based on optical flow. Procedia Eng 15:2201–2205. doi: 10.1016/j.proeng.2011.08.412

114. Madjidi H, Negahdaripour S (2006) On robustness and localization accuracy of optical flow computation for underwater color images. Comput Vis Image Underst 104(1):61–76. doi: 10.1016/j.cviu.2006.07.003

115. Amiaz T, Lubetzky E, Kiryati N (2007) Coarse to over-fine optical flow estimation. Pattern Recognit 40(9):2496–2503. doi:10.1016/j.patcog.2006.09.011

116. Kalmoun EM, Köstler H, Rüde U (2007) 3D optical flow computation using a parallel variational multigrid scheme with application to cardiac C-arm CT motion. Image Vis Comput 25(9):1482–1494. doi:10.1016/j.imavis.2006.12.017

117. Fernández-Caballero A, Castillo JC, Martínez-Cantos J, Martínez-Tomás R (2010) Optical flow or image subtraction in human detection from infrared camera on mobile robot. Robot Auton Syst 58(12):1273–1281. doi:10.1016/j.robot.2010.06.002

118. Karasulu B (2012) The ViCamPEv website. (http://efe.ege.edu.tr/ ~ karasulu/vicampev/). or (http://efe.ege.edu.tr/ karasulu/vicampev/). Accessed 10 May 2012

119. Howlett M (2009) Nplot. Net charting-plotting scientific library. http://www.netcontrols.org/nplot. Accessed 20 Jan 2010

120. Thirde D, Borg M, Aguilera J, Wildenauer H, Ferryman J, Kampel M (2007) Robust real-time tracking for visual surveillance. EURASIP J Adv Signal Process 23. Article ID 96568. doi:10.1155/2007/96568

121. Aguilera J, Wildenauer H, Kampel M, Borg M, Thirde D, Ferryman J (2005) Evaluation of motion segmentation quality for aircraft activity surveillance. In: Proceedings of the 2nd joint IEEE international workshop on visual surveillance and perform (VS-PETS '05), Beijing, China, pp 293–300, 2005. doi:10.1109/VSPETS.2005.1570928

122. Viitaniemi V, Laaksonen J (2007) Evaluating the performance in automatic image annotation: Example case by adaptive fusion of global image features. Signal Process Image Commun 22(6):557–568. doi:10.1016/j.image.2007.05.003

123. Karasulu B (2010) A simulated annealing based performance optimization approach for moving object detection and tracking in videos. Ph.D. Dissertation (in Turkish), Computer Engineering Department, Ege University, Izmir, p 215

Index